For His Glory:

A Kaleidoscope of Wisdom

James (Jim) Barr

Copyright © 2011 James Barr
All rights reserved.
ISBN: 1467930466
ISBN- 13: 978-1467930468

This book is dedicated to:

Our Lord Jesus Christ and all those that love Him.

To him that by wisdom made the heavens: for his mercy endureth for ever. Psalms 136:5

> *But let him that glorieth glory in this, that he understandeth and knoweth me, that I am the LORD which exercise lovingkindness, judgment, and righteousness, in the earth: for in these things I delight, saith the LORD.*
> Jeremiah 9:24
>
> *****
>
> *Happy is the man that findeth wisdom, and the man that getteth understanding.*
> Proverbs 3:13

Table of Contents

PREFACE	VII
SEEING STARS	1
A NEW BATTLE EACH DAY	3
FOUR WORDS THAT CAN CHANGE ANY SITUATION	4
THE QUESTION IS?	5
ACCEPT RESPONSIBILITY	6
OWN UP TO YOUR RESPONSIBILITY!	7
ARE YOU A NERVOUS WRECK?	8
LONG SHADOWS	9
AVOID THE SIN OF WORRY	10
BE A PERSON OF YOUR WORD	11
BE UNSHAKABLE! LEARN TO BOUNCE BACK!	12
BE MORE THAN A DREAMER	13
WORKLESS MYTH	15
BEFRIEND THE WISE	16
BEWARE OF GREEDINESS	18
BEWARE OF PRIDE	20
BIG SKY COUNTRY	21
WHO'S IN CHARGE?	22
CHAINED ROCK	23
CHOOSE THE NOBLE WAY	25
THE HIGH ROAD	26
CONTENTMENT	27
COFFEE CUP MEMORIES	28
CULTIVATE A GOOD WORK ETHIC	29
DIG DEEP	30
CULTIVATE NO EXCUSES	31
CULTIVATE AN EMPATHETIC HEART	33
DEFEATED BEFORE THE BATTLE	36
DISTINGUISHING MARK	39
DISTINGUISHING THE BEST FROM THE GOOD	41
DO RIGHT BY PEOPLE	42
DOUBLE STANDARD?	44
EVERYTHING IS GOING TO BE ALL RIGHT!	45
EYE PROBLEMS	46
GET TO KNOW YOU	47
GUARD MY MOUTH	48
HONEST WEIGHTS	49
I WISH I HAD...	50
LEADERS LEAD	51
LEARN TO BITE YOUR TONGUE	52
LEARN TO FORGIVE	53

Clear Up Misunderstandings Quickly	54
Empty Bitterness	55
Learn to Respect	57
Learn to Love Yourself	58
Accept God's Forgiveness	59
Learn When To Say No!	60
Let's Decorate the Tree or Maybe Not!	63
Lions and Tigers! O My!	65
Live a Disciplined Life	68
Lord! Light My Candle	70
More Work Please	71
Never Give Up	72
Personalize the Promise	74
The Square	78
Prudence	79
Read	80
Woodpecker Wisdom	82
Relationships	83
Self-Worth	84
Speak Encouragement	85
Seek to be Meek!	86
Thank You Lord for Your Patience	87
The Blessings of Having Little	88
The Homeless Child, Jesus	90
The Meaning of Life	91
The Pursuit of ~~Happiness~~ Holiness	92
The Past	95
This is the Year the Lord has Given Us	96
Time to Put the Brakes On!	97
Victory	98
Not By Chance	100
A Whack on the Side of the Head	101
April Makes a Break for It	103
Danger Thin Air	105
Are You In a Hard Way?	107
Clear the Table	108
Cricket Jitters	111
Seven principles of discernment	112
Bully Fish	114
April Wants to Talk	115
Don't Attract the Mosquitoes	117
If You Hang Out A Bird Feeder	119
Unity & Humbleness	120

WHY DO SQUIRRELS PLAY IN THE ROAD?	121
THE WOW IN JESUS' HEALING	122
INFLUENCE!	123
HOPE IN A DARK WORLD	124
RECKLESSNESS AND FAITH	126
ALL THE DAYS IN THE WORLD?	127
ABOUT THE AUTHOR	129

James Barr

All Scripture used in this book is from the King James Bible the 1769 Authorized Version unless otherwise identified.

Scripture quotations marked (NIV) are taken from the Holy Bible, New International Version®, NIV®. Copyright © 1973, 1978, 1984, 2011 by Biblica, Inc.™ Used by permission of Zondervan. All rights reserved worldwide. www.zondervan.com.

Scripture quotations marked (NASB) © are taken from the NEW AMERICAN STANDARD BIBLE®, Copyright © 1960,1962,1963,1968,1971,1972,1973,1975,1977,1995 by The Lockman Foundation. Used by permission. All rights reserved.

Scriptures marked as "(CEV)®" are taken from the Contemporary English Version, Second Edition. Copyright © 2006 by American Bible Society. Used by permission. All rights reserved.

Preface

> So whether you eat or drink or whatever you do, do it all for the glory of God. -1 Corinthians 10:31

God displays His wisdom in the simplest manners.

I cannot put a firm date or time to it; but several years ago, I realized that God's wisdom was being played out before me in everyday events and people. The scriptures that I had read and taught took life in ordinary people and daily events. With this new illumination, came a deep desire to share these little bits of wisdom with others. Spanning several years and using various modes, I began putting to pen the tidbits of biblical wisdom as revealed to me through everyday channels, until now.

For His Glory is more than a devotional book. In some ways, it is autobiographical because it is a collection of lessons revealed through my life experiences. In other ways, For His Glory is a deep theological thesis written for the ordinary person because it reveals the great glory of an awesome God. I prefer to call it a journal of biblical wisdom – basic, practical, easy to read and easily applied to real life. It is a collection of thoughts that can make a big difference in your life. It has in mine.

As a child, I was fascinated with a relatively inexpensive toy called a kaleidoscope. The cardboard tube, looking like a small telescope, could display colorful and beautiful mosaic patterns when you looked into one end and pointed the other end toward a light. Every time, you turned the end pointed toward the light you would get a new pattern and different combination of colors. When the time came to compile these various nuggets of wisdom into this book, I chose to use a kaleidoscope method. I let the nuggets of truth fall where they may and trust that God will let the reader see His glory in His wisdom.

Hence, the reader is not expected to read straight through the book but rather the reader is encouraged to read a thought or two and allow the wisdom revealed to sink deep within his or her heart. The wisdom insights do not need to be read in any order; each is independent of the other.

There have been so many people that have been an encouragement and help in producing this book that I dare not attempt to name them for fear, I would forget someone. I will, however, mention my loving wife, Pat, because without her this would have never gone to press; and the people of Calvary Baptist Church in Bloomington, Indiana, who have been a source of great encouragement.

Lastly, I would like to acknowledge the source of all wisdom – my Lord and my Redeemer, Jesus Christ. For His Glory is written for the sole purpose of glorifying Him.

James (Jim) Barr
Bloomington, IN
October 29, 2011

The wisdom of God devised a way for the love of God to deliver sinners from the wrath of God while not compromising the righteousness of God. -John Piper, Desiring God

For His Glory: A Kaleidoscope of Wisdom

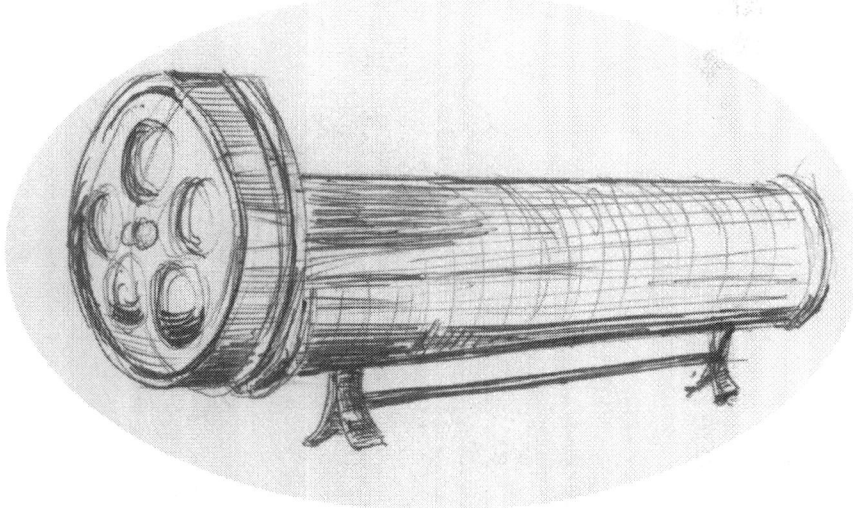

Our thanks to Allen Sullivan for allowing us to use the graphic *Kaleidoscope!*©
Copyright 2011 Allen Sullivan

The word kaleidoscope was formed from combining the Greek words *kalos* "beautiful" and *eidos* "shape" with the English word *scope* by its inventor, Scottish scientist David Brewster. The figurative meaning of the word in the English is "constantly changing pattern." The word is used in the title of this book because the infinite glory of our unchanging God is continuously being revealed through his endless wisdom. Every moment of everyday we can see the wonders of his Glory in the patterns of his wisdom. We only need to look.

Seeing Stars

It was bitterly cold. The only place colder on earth was my heart. I was angry, hurt, and defeated. A cloud of depression and despair hung over my head. The cloudless and moonless drive home promised no relief.

Recklessly, I turned into my driveway spinning my tires and then locking my brakes at the last minute before the driveway ended. Sitting in my car I stewed over the day's events. I dwelled long and hard on the disappointments and the injustices. Where was God, the God, I had pointed others too? Where was the God of glory?

Stepping out of the lukewarm car onto the dry snow, the bitter cold air filled my lungs. The crunching of the snow played the music of my broken heart. I was a shattered man.

Then I looked up.

The clear, cold, dark night was magically alive with countless stars. Vast glorious dots of lights filled the night. Instantly, they took my breath away. Gasping, I sucked in a large breath of cool air making my head swim and knees weak. There – there was the glory of God.

I stood there for several minutes stargazing, awestruck, and suddenly rejuvenated. The cold air was no longer bitter but refreshing. The disappointments, discouragement, and defeat were swallowed by the glory of creation. The world wasn't out of control. I was.

According to a team of stargazers based at the Australian National University, there are about 70 sextillion stars. That's a 7 followed by 22 zeros! Each of those stars is placed exactly where God chose by His wisdom. Who was I to question His wisdom or His ways?

All of creation declares the wisdom and glory of God. If the stars, all 70 sextillion of them, are placed in the universe for his glory, then I too am here to glorify God. Glorify Him, I will do through his grace and by living according to His wisdom.

Lord, please grant your servant wisdom. Amen.

A New Battle Each Day

At the start of each day, a new battle begins. It is the battle for your time and devotion. The two go hand-in-hand. There can be no devotion without time, and time must accompany devotion. Therefore, each morning a battle for our time and devotion begins.

Our time in prayer and scripture reading do not always win the battle. The matters of the day or the troublesome problems of the night can crowd out our "quiet time" – our time for prayer and meditation. We put the urgent before the important, the pressing before the essential. This is a formula for defeat. When we allow the urgent to rob us of the essential time needed with our Lord, we will be ill-prepared for the next pressing problem of the day and the next urgent matter.

The real battle of the day is either won or lost in those early-morning hours when we choose to spend time with God in prayer and meditation, or we choose not too.

And in the morning, rising up a great while before day, he went out, and departed into a solitary place, and there prayed. -Mark 1:35

"I have so much to do that I shall spend the first three hours in prayer." — Martin Luther

Wisdom Snippet

There is great wisdom to be found in alone time with God. Take time to be alone with God. With Bible in hand and an attitude of prayer, get alone with God.

Four Words That Can Change Any Situation...

Take time to pray. These four words can change any situation and any life – including your own. Prayer opens the communication channels with God and taps the power of the creator of the universe. Again, I say, "Take time to pray."

"Some of us let the hurry of our lives crowd prayer out, and what a waste of time and energy and nerve force there is by the constant worry! One night of prayer will save us from many nights of insomnia. Time spent in prayer is not wasted, but time invested..."
-R. A. TORREY, How to Pray

"The men who have done the most for God in this world have been early on their knees. He who fritters away the early morning, its opportunity and freshness, in other pursuits than seeking God will make poor headway seeking Him the rest of the day. If God is not first in our thoughts and efforts in the morning, He will be in the last place the remainder of the day." -E. M. Bounds

"When a Christian shuns fellowship with other Christians, the devil smiles. When he stops studying the Bible, the devil laughs. When he stops praying, the devil shouts for joy." -Corrie Ten Boom

The Question Is?

Several years ago a cartoon appeared in *the Saturday Review of Literature* in which young George Washington was standing with an ax in his hand. Before him, lying on the ground was the famous cherry tree. He had already made his smug admission that he had done it - after all, he "...cannot tell a lie." Nevertheless, his father was standing there, exasperated, saying, "All right, so you admit it! You always admit it! The question is, when are you going to stop doing it?"

The growing problem facing Christianity today is not how to get people to own up to sin, although that still remains a task; but rather how to get them to stop from returning to sin. Lost in the shuffle of religious terms is the true meaning of repentance – a change of mind, a turning from one direction to another.

Most people do not like to dwell on the horrors of the crucifixion. It is too bloody, too horrible. The crucifixion is the flawless picture of just how ugly sin is. You would think that if anything could help us turn from our sin; it would be a clear and perfect view of the horror of sin and its cost. Even so, the horrors of the cross and all of its ugliness of the crucifixion are not what turn men from their sin. It is the goodness of God seen in the sacrifice of the Son that leads people to repent: "...not knowing that the goodness of God leadeth thee to repentance?" (Romans 2:4).

It is the act of love and not the fear of punishment that draws people to Christ. Grace is the contrast between the law and the cross. Grace always wins because God's grace "is sufficient" (2 Corinthians 12:9).

Accept Responsibility

The date was October 15, 1962. A packet of photos was delivered to his hand. Perhaps the words of a former President played in his mind as he viewed the photos. What had Truman said? "The buck stops here."

The world was literally on the brink of nuclear war, and the responsibility for a nation fell on him. Soviet missiles were being deployed in Cuba. For the first time, the Soviets would be capable of dropping nuclear missiles on the mainland of the United States. President John F. Kennedy would shoulder the responsibility of guiding a nation through the most dangerous third world war threat in modern history.

He did so by accepting the responsibility entrusted to him.

Man must cease attributing his problems to his environment, and learn again to exercise his will - his personal responsibility in the realm of faith and morals. –Albert Schweitzer

For it is written, As I live, saith the Lord, every knee shall bow to me, and every tongue shall confess to God. So then every one of us shall give account of himself to God.
                                                      Romans 14:11-12

Own Up to Your Responsibility!

Own up to your responsibility! Don't run from it. You cannot outrun it. Don't hide from it. It will always find you. Embrace it and accept it.

Don't try to shift blame or excuse your mistakes. Take responsibility for your blunders. Seek to rectify any error quickly then let go of it.

Learn to forgive yourself. Past mistakes must not haunt the "now" nor affect the "future." They will not if you do not allow them too.

> The thorns which I have reap'd are of the tree
> I planted; they have torn me, and I bleed.
> I should have known what fruit would spring from such a seed.
> ~George Gordon, *Lord Byron, Childe Harold's Pilgrimage*

The most important thought that ever occupied my mind is that of my individual responsibility to God. - Daniel Webster

Are You A Nervous Wreck?

April is our beagle and is, by nature, a lovable dog. Nevertheless, she has two qualities that drive me up a tree. Her bark can make the hair on the back of your neck stand straight up; and she becomes a nervous wreck in thunder storms.

When a storm is approaching, April goes wild. She shakes, whimpers, and she barks until everyone is aware that a storm is approaching. No matter what you do, nothing will ease her fears or calm her nerves. She is miserable and so are you!

Some people are a lot like April only it's not the physical storms they fear but the storms of life. They fear of failure, or acceptance, or disease, or any number of things makes them miserable; and they make everyone around them miserable! In the KJV translation of the Bible, the term "fear not" appears 63 times including the comforting words spoken in Luke 12:32: "Fear not, little flock; for it is your Father's good pleasure to give you the Kingdom." No matter what life may throw at you, the believer has the assurance that he or she is part of the Lord's flock. The Christian has little to fear in this world "because greater is he that is in you, than he that is in the world" (1 John 4:4).

The same Jesus that calmed the storm for his disciples is available to claim the fears that are making you miserable.

Casting all your care upon him; for he careth for you.
-1 Peter 5:7

When it thunders, the thief becomes honest. -English Proverb

Long Shadows

The evening sky was extremely dark last night. Normally Toby, our dog, is totally oblivious to the night; but this evening, for reasons only known to the pup, he was more than a little jumpy. The single porch light causes Toby and me to cast some extremely long shadows that only added to the eerie feelings of the night. As we walked and our shadows proceeded with us, Toby's anxiety grew.

Toby's uneasiness also had an infectious effect on me. Normal night sounds became amplified; and with each bump in the night, I felt the hair on the back of my neck stand up. Toby and I were feeding our fear frenzy. As I became unnerved, he became unnerved; and the more panic-stricken he became, the more panic-stricken I became until we both decided to head to the safety of the house.

Once inside, I reflected on this phenomenon. There was nothing different that night than any other evening other than the fact that Toby was uneasy. I picked up on his uneasiness and allowed the shadows and sounds of the evening to touch my fears and fire up my feeler. Once my emotions shot upward, Toby's senses heightened, and soon we were producing our own nightmare out of nothing.

Often in life we feed each other's fears, when there really is nothing to fear. Someone will complain of a pain in the side, and before you know it someone has them dying of cancer. The weather will look stormy, and someone will turn it into a man-eating twister. A business will close; and before the day is up, someone will have us in the Great Depression. Believers need to be careful not to become fear mongrels but rather to be encouragers that place their trust and fears in the hands of the Lord.

Avoid the Sin of Worry

Avoid the sin of worrying. Yes, worrying is a sin. If you are worried about something that you have control over, then change it. If you are worried about something that you have no control over, then it belongs to God. Trust Him! Practice this simple principle:

> Be careful for nothing; but in every thing by prayer and supplication with thanksgiving let your requests be made known unto God. - Philippians 4:6

"Worry does not empty tomorrow of its sorrow. It empties today of its strength." -Corrie Ten Boom

---

Wisdom Snippet
"We sometimes fear to bring our troubles to God, because they must seem small to Him who *sitteth on the circle of the earth*. But if they are large enough to vex and endanger our welfare, they are large enough to touch His heart of love. For love does not measure by a merchant's scales, not with a surveyor's chain. It hath a delicacy... unknown in any handling of material substance." - R. A. Torrey

Be a Person of Your Word.

People destroy their testimony and tarnish their character because they rush into commitments – commitments that they have every intention of fulfilling when they are made but often are undoable. Their intentions are good, but the results are bad. Before you make any commitment make sure you can keep the commitment. If you say, "yes" - then yes it is! However, "no" is often the right answer and the mature reply.

Life is full of uncertainties that can make even the most prudent person fail. Therefore, it is wise to choose only those commitments that are in the will of the Lord, and that you are willing to make great sacrifices in order to honor your word. Choose to commit only to those that are important and be careful of those that are urgent. Then, above all else, to the best of your ability be a person of your word.

He who guards his lips guards his life, but he who speaks rashly will come to ruin. -Proverbs 13:3

But let your communication be, Yea, yea; Nay, nay: for whatsoever is more than these cometh of evil. Matthew 5:37

We must not promise what we ought not, lest we be called on to perform what we cannot. -Abraham Lincoln

Promise little and do much. ~Hebrew Proverb

Be Unshakable! Learn to Bounce Back!

Resilience and steadiness are two characteristics of an unshakable person!

Never before had a man been so tested. He was a good man who led an upright life. God even referred to him as a righteous man. However, in a matter of hours, enormous tragedy wiped out all that he held precious. In a catastrophic accident, he lost all of his children and all of his wealth. If that wasn't bad enough, he would lose his health; followed by what might have been the hardest blow, he would lose the respect of his wife and his closest friends. In the days to follow, Job would have to dig down deep and examine his life closely to find the strength to be an unshakable man – a man who would bounce back. What made him so resilient and steadfast? Probably, the qualities found in this Psalm of David:

LORD, who may dwell in your sanctuary? Who may live on your holy hill? He whose walk is blameless and who does what is righteous, who speaks the truth from his heart and has no slander on his tongue, who does his neighbor no wrong and casts no slur on his fellowman, who despises a vile man but honors those who fear the LORD, who keeps his oath even when it hurts, who lends his money without usury and does not accept a bribe against the innocent. He who does these things will never be shaken. Psalm 15 (NIV)

Be More Than a Dreamer

> He who works his land will have abundant food,
> but he who chases fantasies lacks judgment.
> Proverbs 12:11 (NIV)

Joseph had a dream. It was from God, and Joseph knew it. His dream told him that one day he would be a great ruler, so prominent a ruler that his family would bow down to him. Of course, his life and his dream took many turns before his dream became a reality. Sold into slavery by his brothers, carried off to a strange country, and falsely imprisoned, Joseph had many chances to abandon his vision. Joseph could have been the guy who said, "When life gives you lemons then make lemonade." He did his best, never forgot who he was, and at no time abandoned his dream or his God. It took years, but his dream became a reality because Joseph was more than a dreamer.

Dreams are good but only when they are put into action. Pages and pages of dreams are recorded in heaven, but only a few come to birth. A dream becomes a reality when it is embraced with conviction, sweat, and fear.

A dream cannot grow unless it is planted in the soil of conviction. Christopher Columbus had a dream that was planted in conviction. It did not disappear with rejection nor did it fade when his voyage became long and difficult. Columbus believed in this dream. He embraced his dream with deep certainty. Most dreams do not come to reality because the dreamer doesn't believe in it.

Like a plant, a dream will not produce without cultivation. No farmer will survive without cultivating what he has planted.

The dreamer who is not willing to put sweat behind his dream will always remain a dreamer but never a doer.

Sometimes the hardest work does not appear in the actual "doing" of the dream but in preparation; the homework required before you can even start. Columbus had to know how to command a ship before he set sail. Many a dream has been lost because of poor preparation. Even more dreams are lost because the dreamer didn't have the conviction to prepare for the task ahead. He or she was defeated before they began.

Every dream has an element of risk. As the days drew long and the food ran short, Columbus' conviction met head-on with his fears. Fears, especially the fear of failure, can cause you to abandon your dream. Yes, chasing a dream can end in failure! However, not pursuing a dream will always end in failure! Dreamers who wish to see their dream become a reality must be willing to accept the risk and do the work.

Workless Myth

He becometh poor that dealeth with a slack hand: but the hand of the diligent maketh rich. Proverbs 10:4

Wealth without work is a myth. This mindset has wrecked the potential of many a good person. Today, there is a complete industry, which is working very hard and becoming excessively prosperous, trying to convince you that all you really need is the right break. The wedge these get-rich-quick schemes have is they sell you your dreams; but never tell you that the only way those dreams become reality is by working – usually very hard.

Here is a simple question I ask myself when deciding if something is to-good-to-be-true: If you could really make that much money that easily, wouldn't everybody be doing it?

Don't spend your life trying to buy your dreams while making someone else rich. Spend your life working for those dreams.

I do not know anyone who has gotten to the top without hard work. That is the recipe. It will not always get you to the top, but it will get you pretty near. ~Margaret Thatcher

Befriend the Wise

He who walks with the wise grows wise...
                                        Proverbs 13:20 (NIV)

He had some big shoes to fill and an over-taxed nation to lead. His first challenge after becoming king would test his character and challenge his wisdom. Rehoboam would be approached by the northern tribes of Israel with a request to lower the burden his father, King Solomon, had placed on the people. What would he do?

Asking for three days to consider the request, Rehoboam sought counsel first from the older-and-wiser counselors of his father, which instructed him to heed to the request of the people. All would have gone well had he listened to those senior counselors but the recommendation they gave didn't settle well with Rehoboam. He proceeded to seek advice from his younger friends; people who knew what he wanted to hear and who thought themselves wiser than their forefathers.

The result was a civil war and a divided nation. Rehoboam had surrounded himself with fools and not with tested people of wisdom.

Wisdom is found in godly people. You will not find good judgment in a fool. Befriend the prudent. "Hang with" those that are proven to be wise or judicious. If you do, then you will grow in wisdom and intellect.

When searching for an astute person, remember Solomon's warning. Wisdom always begins with the fear of the Lord – the reverent and awesome respect for the Almighty. Never take advice or model your life after someone who is not walking with the Lord. Seek out the aged, the seasoned people that have earned their undergraduate degree from experience and their doctorate from hard knocks.

Stay away from a foolish man, for you will not find knowledge on his lips. -Proverbs 14:7 (NIV)

A wise man can see more from the bottom of a well than a fool can from a mountain top. -Author Unknown

> **Wisdom Snippet**
>
> *Listen to God! Solomon sought wisdom, and God granted him his wish until he turned from God and listened to others. Wisdom, true wisdom, is found in His Word. Let the Bible be your guide.*

Beware of Greediness

"Watch out! Be on your guard against all kinds of greed..." - Jesus (Luke 12:15 NIV)

A tight fist around even a dollar can be deadly.

Charles Swindoll gives a good account of just how deadly it can be in his book *Living Above the Level of Mediocrity*:

> *Men who trap animals in Africa for zoos in America say that one of the hardest animals to catch is the ringtail monkey. For the Zulus of that continent, however, it's simple. They've been catching this agile little animal with ease for years. The method the Zulus use is based on knowledge of the animal. Their trap is nothing more than a melon growing on a vine. The seeds of this melon are a favorite of the monkey. Knowing this, the Zulus simply cut a hole in the melon, just large enough for the monkey to insert his hand to reach the seeds inside. The monkey will stick his hand in, grab as many seeds as he can, then start to withdraw it. This he cannot do. His fist is now larger than the hole. The monkey will pull and tug, screech and fight the melon for hours. Nevertheless, he can't get free of the trap, unless he gives up the seeds, which he refuses to do. Meanwhile, the Zulus sneak up and nab him.* (Charles Swindoll, Living Above the Level of Mediocrity, p.150ff.)

Greed can take control of your life; and it can be an all-consuming drive that will warp your perspective on life. Greed has destroyed marriages and homes, businesses and churches; and it has driven many a person to a miserable life and an early grave.

But perhaps the most destructive quality of greed is that it can come disguised in many subtle ways. Greed does not always desire material positions or money. Greed can desire fame, power, and control. It is best described as coveting – an unhealthy yearning or craving. Be on the look out! Beware of greed!

He is no fool who gives what he cannot keep to gain what he cannot lose. -Jim Elliot

Wisdom Snippet

Money never made a man happy yet, nor will it. There is nothing in its nature to produce happiness. The more a man has, the more he wants. Instead of filling a vacuum, it makes one.
Benjamin Franklin

Beware of Pride

Be proud of what the Lord has done but beware of self-glorifying pride. Pride has brought the mightiest of men down. Seek to make every endeavor an endeavor for the Lord. (And whatsoever ye do, do *it* heartily, as to the Lord, and not unto men; - Col 3:23) Be quick to acknowledge the credit others deserve. Do not toot your own horn. The sound that will come forth will be sour in the ears of the hearer. Let these two proverbs become the principles you live by:

Let another man praise thee, and not thine own mouth; a stranger, and not thine own lips. -Proverbs 27:2

It is not good to eat much honey: so *for men* to search their own glory *is not* glory. -Proverbs 25:27

Pride is Deceitful

Pride has caused many to fall.

Pride can cause us to lose the proper perspective in almost any situation.

Pride can lead to sin and rebellion as it did Satan. It can also cause us to remain in sin keeping us from confessing our sin.

Pride is so deceitful that we often don't realize it has a hold on us.

Search your heart carefully and do not let pride be your downfall.

Big Sky Country

All of my life I have heard the term "Big Sky Country" and never understood it until a recent trip through the flat plains of northwest Illinois. This farmland is among some of the most productive farmland in the world. Its flat terrain allows you to see miles in any direction. Looking out across the land, you would see a magnificent landscape picture of which about eighty-percent is sky – therefore, the expression "Big Sky Country."

While admiring the view of distant barns slightly rising above the horizon and the wonder of a bright blue sky with puffs of pillow-like clouds, the thought came to me about how we should see more of *the above* rather than fretting about *the things below*.

Far too often we run in a rut of our own making and soon forget about the big picture. Forgetting that God is Sovereign and very much in control of all things, we fasten our eyes on immediate earthly problems and miss the joy of heaven and our future hope.

Set your minds on things above, not on earthly things.
                              -Colossians 3:2 (NIV)

"God is God. Because He is God, He is worthy of my trust and obedience. I will find rest nowhere but in His holy will, a will that is unspeakably beyond my largest notions of what He is up to."
-Elisabeth Elliot, the wife of slain missionary Jim Elliot

Who's in Charge?

Never forget and always acknowledge the fact that God is in command. He always is! There is nothing that is not in his control. Although we may not understand all His ways, we must trust in His love and accept His will. Trust is not always easy; but if you allow God, He will embrace you with this love and gently guide you through.

Thou shalt guide me with thy counsel, and afterward receive me to glory. -Psalm 73:24

"You have trusted Him in a few things, and He has not failed you. Trust Him now for everything, and see if He does not do for you exceeding abundantly above all that you could ever have asked or thought, not according to your power or capacity, but according to His own mighty power, that will work in you all the good pleasure of His most blessed will. You find no difficulty in trusting the Lord with the management of the universe and all the outward creation, and can your case be any more complex or difficult than these, that you need to be anxious or troubled about His management of it?"
-Hannah Whitall Smith

> *...incline thine ear unto wisdom, and apply thine heart to understanding; For the LORD giveth wisdom: out of his mouth cometh knowledge and understanding.*
> Proverbs 2:2, 6

Chained Rock

Nestled in a valley in the Appalachian Mountains is the small community of Pineville, Kentucky. Each morning the residents of Pineville awake to the majestic sight of mountains of which none is more awesome than Pine Mountain. Near the Peak of Pine Mountain is also another awesome but alarming sight. In view of the entire town below is an enormous boulder hanging on the edge of the mountain waiting for the right moment to let loose and come crashing down on the village below. Although this may or may not be possible, the appearance definitely appears to be possible. This explains the massive chain wrapped around and fastened to the boulder giving Pineville its famed tourist sight, Chained Rock.

> "God has wisely kept us in the dark concerning future events and reserved for himself the knowledge of them, that he may train us up in a dependence upon himself and a continued readiness for every event." - Matthew Henry

The idea of waking up every morning with a huge rock over my head might cause me to seek some way of securing the rock too. However, after seeing the chain and seeing the rock, I have my doubts that if the earth shook and the boulder let loose the chain would hold the boulder.

Each of us awakes to a majestic world that God has created. You do not need to live in mountains to see the majesty of God's creation. Even so, we also live under a boulder of uncertainty. There are a number of unknown possibilities that could come crashing down on us at any time. We can attempt to limit uncertainties like the people of Pineville did by holding them back; but there is no real assurance that we, in our own strength and ingenuity, can do so.

What we can do and what we should do is seek the refuge and protection found in the Rock of Ages. Only the Lord can sustain us and give us the strength to withstand the uncertainties of life. The Lord alone is our assurance that no matter what happens, He holds our hand and eternity is our home. Put your faith in the Lord and not the chain of your own might.

Trust in the LORD with all thine heart; and lean not unto thine own understanding. Proverb 3:5

The fear of man bringeth a snare: but whoso putteth his trust in the LORD shall be safe. Proverbs 29:25

"God will never, never, never let us down if we have faith and put our trust in Him. He will always look after us. So we must cleave to Jesus. Our whole life must simply be woven into Jesus."
-Mother Teresa

Get Out of the Way!

Allow God to bless you. God wishes to bless us but often we get in the way by trying to help him. Get out of the way! God doesn't need our help but He does demand our total surrender to Him and His will. Remember God's answer to the Apostle Paul, "My grace is sufficient for thee: for my strength is made perfect in weakness (2Co 12:9).

Choose the Noble Way

When Abram (i.e. Abraham) learned that his relative, Lot, had been carried off captive along with all of Lot's wealth, Abram came to the rescue.

Earlier, Lot, Abram's nephew, had chosen to live in the pleasant plains of Sodom leaving his uncle the rough mountainous land. Abram could have delighted in Lot's demise; but with the help of three other tribes, Abram perused the victors and defeated them, freeing Lot and all the captives.

Having recovered all the loot, Abram could have kept it but chose to take the noble way and returned it to the freed captives with the exception of giving the Lord a tithe and rewarding those tribes that fought with him.

He took the noble way.

The High Road

Take the high road. If it's questionable, a choice between definitely right and maybe right, always choose what you know to be right. The high road is often more difficult and demanding, but it will never lead you into the deep sewer waters of sin.

"...choose you this day whom ye will serve..." Joshua 24:15

I know that there is nothing better for men than to be happy and do good while they live. Ecclesiastes 3:12

Contentment

While reading through the book of Numbers, I began to wonder if Moses ever got tired of the whining. For a nation of people that had firsthand seen the power and wonders of the Lord, Israel was a whiny bunch.

Contentment seems to be a word that is quickly disappearing from the life of many. Slowly and deceitfully, we have allowed the planting of seeds of discontentment in our hearts.

Perhaps we need to revisit Hebrew 13:5:

> Keep your lives free from the love of money and be content with what you have, because God has said, "Never will I leave you; never will I forsake you."

Lord, please allow us to swim in the pool of contentment and not bathe in the pool of self-pity.

But godliness with contentment is great gain. -1Timothy 6:6

Rest in the Lord

Rest in the Lord. WHEN YOU ARE RIGHT WITH GOD ALL IS AT PEACE. Trust Him and relax. God is in control. Daniel could sleep with the lions because he trusted his God. The three children of Israel could stroll in the fire because they walked with the Lord. Paul could sing while in prison because he rested with the Lord. Trust Him and relax!

Coffee Cup Memories

Then ye shall answer them, That the waters of Jordan were cut off before the ark of the covenant of the LORD; when it passed over Jordan, the waters of Jordan were cut off: and these stones shall be for a memorial unto the children of Israel for ever. - Joshua 4:7

Setting before me is a coffee cup complete with hot coffee, which has fond memories. The cup itself is not worth much, but the memories are priceless. It was purchased a few years ago, when Pat and I camped in Texas on our way to the Grand Canyon. We packed our car full, loaded our only dog at the time, and started an adventure that we look back on with pleasant thoughts. Like most campers, we thought we'd brought everything we would ever need only to find that we had no cups for our morning coffee. Thus, the souvenir coffee cups.

It is funny how little things can cause warmhearted memories and bring a smile to your face. They remind you to be thankful for blessings that God has bestowed on you. Such was the reason why the Israelites were to pick up twelve stones out of the riverbed of the Jordon when they crossed into the Promised Land. The stones were to be used to build a memorial so that future generations could remember how God had parted the waters of Jordan for His people.

It is a good idea that God's people build some spiritual memories in their life to remind them of what God has done for them. Take a moment and look around your home and see what spiritual memories you can find and join with me in thanking the Lord.

Cultivate a Good Work Ethic

His mother was a black slave, and his father was a white farmer from a nearby town. His first experience to education was carrying the books for his master's daughter as she went off to school. After the Emancipation Proclamation of 1865 and relocating in West Virginia, he took a job in the salt mine starting at 4 a.m. so he could attend school later in the day. Reinforcing his belief in the dignity of hard work he would write, "From the time that I can remember anything, almost every day of my life has been occupied in some kind of labor."

Booker T. Washington would become an American political leader, educator, orator, author and one of the most influential African-American leaders of his day. He did so by cultivating a good work ethic and not allowing circumstances or his environment to become an excuse.

If a person desires too, they can always find an excuse to avoid work. Proverbs plainly states "The slothful man saith, 'There is a lion in the way; a lion is in the streets" (Proverbs 26:13).

"Success is not measured by the position one has reached in life, rather by the obstacles one overcomes while trying to succeed"
-Booker T. Washington

> *Ninety-nine percent of the failures come from people who have the habit of making excuses.*
> -George Washington Carver

Dig Deep

Are you a scripture surfer? Are you one of those people that occasionally pick a Bible up expecting to read it like a novel? Then when you find the character's names are strange, and the content is foreign you quickly lay it aside saying it's too hard to understand. This might shock you, but the scriptures are not too hard to understand. You are too lazy!

R.C. Sproul stated it correctly when he said, "We fail in our duty to study God's Word not so much because it is difficult to understand, not so much because it is dull and boring, but because it is work. Our problem is not a lack of intelligence or a lack of passion. Our problem is that we are lazy."

The scriptures address the deepest questions of the universe and reveal the deep things of an almost incomprehensible God. Do you expect to skim through the Bible and pull out all the nuggets of truth without study?

A seamstress will first study a pattern lest her sewing be in vain. A mechanic would study an auto manual before trying to fix an unknown problem with an engine. Shouldn't a person study the Word of God for the answers to life's deepest questions?

> Study to shew thyself approved unto God, a workman that needeth not to be ashamed, rightly dividing the word of truth. -2 Timothy 2:15

Cultivate No Excuses.

Cultivate a good work ethic and not a bunch of excuses. It will build your self-respect and earn the respect of others. Former baseball outfielder Sam Ewing, put it this way, "Hard work spotlights the character of people: some turn up their sleeves, some turn up their noses, and some don't turn up at all."

Become known as a Doer! Be known as someone that is both wanting and willing to work. When a chore lies before you, do not procrastinate. Be a person of action.

Be known as the person that will tackle the tough jobs and see them through. Be the guy who finishes what you start and never leave anything partially done.

Learn to work alone as well as work with others. Never have anyone work "for" you but rather have them work "with" you. They and you will be more productive when the task is tackled as a team.

> Let this principle be your guide in developing a good work ethic:
>
> Whatsoever thy hand findeth to do, do it with thy might
> —Ecclesiastes 9:10

Wisdom Snippet

Approach today with great expectations for you do not know what great things your Lord has planned for you. Rest assured that those things are for your good. They can only be found by being obedient to God's will and God's word. Face today with enthusiasm and excitement for your Lord has given you this day!

Cultivate an Empathetic Heart

Next to the king, he held the highest position in the nation. He had the awesome obligation of representing the people before God; and the terrifying task of entering into the presence of God with the atonement for the sins of a nation.

Yearly he would get decked out in his fancy garments and enter in the Holy of Holies behind the cherubim veil. Bells were attached to the hem of his garment that would jingle as he moved within the room that held the Ark of the Covenant with its Mercy Seat. As long as the bells tinkled, those outside knew that he was performing his duties exactly as commanded by God; for if he strayed just a little, the punishment would be swift and fatal. God allowed no errors.

The High Priest of Israel, with all his enormous privileges and powers, also carried a tremendous responsibility. Among those responsibilities was to have an empathetic heart.

Bible says:

> Every high priest is selected from among men and is appointed to represent them in matters related to God, to offer gifts and sacrifices for sins. He is able to deal gently with those who are ignorant and are going astray, since he himself is subject to weakness. This is why he has to offer sacrifices for his own sins, as well as for the sins of the people (Hebrews 5:1-3 NIV).

Did you take note of the second verse? "He is able to deal gently with those who are ignorant and are going astray, since he himself is subject to weakness." According to the dictionary, empathy is identification with or vicarious experiencing of the feelings, thoughts, or attitudes of another person. In other words, empathy is walking in the shoes of another person.

It is through empathy that we can really connect with people. Only when we are able to identify with another person can we make good assessments or judgments. Only then are we more likely to have compassion and show mercy. And only then can we come alongside a person and be a comfort and encourager. Cultivate an empathic heart. It will change your relationship with others dramatically.

Love Is Like A Mighty Oak

Love is like a mighty oak. It can weather the storms of life and withstand the heat of opposition. But even the mighty oak must be watered to live. Love must be nurtured to survive and grow. Nurture your love for your spouse, your children, your family, your friends, your neighbor, and above all for your Lord.

Defeated Before the Battle

For months the leak around the bathroom faucet-handle had haunted me. I had even brought the replacement fixture but the challenge of tearing into this plumbing repair was a battle that I greatly feared. I knew the house was old, that a wall would need to be removed, and that I had a very dismal record of working on anything remotely associated with plumbing. I also knew that I could not afford the price of a professional.

Early, one morning, I faced my fears and undertook the task before me. To my surprise, I finished the dreaded chore by noon. The battle that could have been fought months earlier was over; and I was victorious!

I recall an event recorded in the Bible. Israel, under the leadership of King Saul, was faced with a dreadful challenge by an opposing enemy that had a champion named Goliath. When faced with having to fight this nine-foot giant and the taunts of their enemies, Saul and his army were frozen with fright.

When Saul and all Israel heard those words of the Philistine, they were dismayed, and greatly afraid. -1 Samuel 17:11

And all the men of Israel, when they saw the man, fled from him, and were sore afraid. -1 Samuel 17:24

I am not one of those people that believe everything can be overcome by "positive thinking." However, clearly, a battle can be lost before the fighting begins because the soldiers have allowed the enemy to defeat them in their heart and mind.

The Philistines and Goliath had already defeated the Israelites without shooting one arrow or delivering one blow. The leaky faucet defeated me before I had touched a wrench. Why? Because I was defeated before the battle!

How many times did you awaken to a new day and had already predestined the day to be a bad day and proved yourself right?

I am persuaded that we give the devil too many victories in our life simply because we allow ourselves to believe we have already lost! We fail because we are defeated from the beginning. We lose the battle in our hearts and our head.

Champions are those that believe they can be victorious and enter the battle believing they can win!

For as he thinketh in his heart, so is he… - Proverbs 23:7

I can do all things through Christ which strengtheneth me. - Philippians 4:13

Yes! You Can!

Do not let the devil or the world deceive you into believing you are trapped or predestined to a certain way of life. God has the power and he will grant the grace to change you and any state of affairs you may find yourself. There only two requirements. You must be willing to change and seek by faith his help.

Distinguishing Mark

And the men said unto her (Rahab), We *will be* blameless of this thine oath which thou hast made us swear. Behold, *when* we come into the land, thou shalt bind this line of scarlet thread in the window which thou didst let us down by: and thou shalt bring thy father, and thy mother, and thy brethren, and all thy father's household, home unto thee. - Jos 2:17-18

Rahab had proven she was a believer in the only Almighty God to the two spies. Because of faith, Rahab's home would be spared. A distinctive red cord hung out her window. Because of that red cord, she and her family would find grace.

Is there a cord? A distinguishing mark that declares your home is a Christian home? Is it visible to all? A home, where the Lord Jesus rules and resides, should be remarkably different than that of a non-believing world. A red cord may not be hanging from your window; but there should be a noticeable difference.

A Christian home is a home where the deep love for God spills over into a deep and sincere love between family members. Family members should be able to depend on it. Christian love is one of the few things in this world that can be a noticeable difference. Love is what separates Christians as followers of Christ.

> By this shall all men know that ye are my disciples,
> if ye have love one to another. - John 13:35.

Love is the fiber of the cord that distinguishes the family who makes Jesus their Lord. Is this kind of love shared in your home?

Love & Safety

Love and safety are two gifts every living thing desire. When you provide an environment where unconditional love (selfless love) can be found, and safety is assured, you can always count on a positive result. This is true with children and spouses! By giving enormous amounts of unselfish love and by being consistent with providing an atmosphere of safety you will develop great relationships.

Distinguishing the Best from the Good

I hate painting! Again, I hate to paint and having said that, with paint still on my hands; this dutiful husband has finished painting a room in our home. Fortunately, my wife and I agreed that the same color that was on the walls before would be the color I would use.

There are some real advantages to using the same color paint. They blend easier. It is simpler to cover. Therefore, you might get by with just one coat.

There are also some disadvantages. One disadvantage is that in places where there are fewer scuff marks, it is sometimes hard to see where you have painted and where you have not.

The same problem occurs occasionally when it comes to distinguishing between what is good and what is best. It is good for me to help others but not at the expense of ignoring the needs of my family. It is good for me to read my Bible but not while I'm being paid to work for someone else. These examples are easy to distinguish; but in real life, the good and the best can be difficult to differentiate.

When painting a white room with white paint, the difference between what has been painted and what hasn't been painted can be tricky. Choosing what is best from what is good can also be difficult. The history of the human race has revealed that discernment or good judgment has not been our strong points – just ask Adam and Eve! We have and still make poor choices; and at times, let the good override the best. Discernment – good judgment – can only be obtained with the help of the Lord. That is why every Morning Prayer should contain this plea: "Teach me good discernment and knowledge..." (Psalms 119:65 NASB)

Do Right By People

Standing an inch over six feet tall and weighing less than one hundred and fifty pounds, he wasn't an impressive man. He was an orphan, whose father had died before his birth, and whose mother died in his early teens. He had a reputation for being a scoundrel as a young man. Nevertheless, with all this going against him, he was a beloved figure to many.

Ordered by the US government to mobilize his volunteer militia and march them to Natchez, Mississippi only to arrive and be told they were no longer needed. At that point, the lean man from Tennessee would choose to do the right thing. He would do right by his men.

Many of his men were sick from the long journey. He rejected the orders to disband and abandon his militia and instead resolved to keep them together – vowing that no man would be left behind. Ordering his officers to surrender their horses to the sick; and setting the example by doing so himself, he led his men home. During the long trek home, his men would find strength and courage as Old Hickory led the way.

Andrew Jackson would become the seventh President of the United States and change American politics forever. The common American would see him as a man that did right by the people. Despite the fact that Jackson had many questionable qualities, the choice he made to do right regardless of personal consequences helped a nation fall in love with him.

Continued

Always do the right thing for others! The Golden rule, "Do unto others as you would have them do unto you" applies today. Don't try to find a way around it or an excuse for not following it. Just do it! Always do right by people. You will find favor with God and earn the respect of people by doing so.

> "Let no pleasure tempt thee, no profit allure thee, no persuasion move thee, to do anything which thou knowest to be evil; so shalt thou always live jollity; for a good conscience is a continual Christmas." -Benjamin Franklin

Double Standard?

Does the average person live by a double standard? Does he or she hold one standard for others and another for themself? This amusing piece of humor reinforces an affirmative answer to our questions:

> The minister's phone rang in his study. A voice, which he recognized as one of his parishioners, said, "Send me six cases of beer."
>
> "Dear lady," said the minister, "this is your pastor."
>
> He expected an apology. But, not believing that she had misdialed, the lady asked indignantly, "Indeed! And what are you doing at a Brewery?"

As comical as that seems, in reality, far too many people hold one standard for themselves and a completely different standard for others. It would be wise to take a moment and remember that God uses the same standard for all.

"Consistency is the foundation of virtue." -Francis Bacon

Thus he shewed me: and, behold, the Lord stood upon a wall made by a plumbline, with a plumbline in his hand. -Amos 7:7

Differing weights and differing measures — the LORD detests them both. -Proverbs 20:10 (NIV)

Everything Is Going To Be All Right!

April, our beagle, is one laid back hound dog unless there is a thunderstorm. Then she is a nervous wreck. Shaking like a leaf, the thirty-four-pound dog will jump into bed with you putting her paws on your chest to let you know that a storm is approaching long before it arrives. No matter what you do, she will not settle down.

A few nights ago, a sensational storm came rolling through when we were camping in our popup tent-camper. This particular storm put on a good display of fireworks, including some sonic booms that shook everything. Needless to say April was beside herself!

With April laying on my chest and heavily panting in my face, I tried to calm her down by patting her head and saying, "Everything is going to be all right." I know that we often credit our dogs with more intelligence than they really have; but I had not gotten the words out of my mouth when April's facial expression and her big brown eyes replied, "Who are you trying to kid! If you have the power to make it right, then calm the storm!"

April was right. I don't have the power to stop storms. In fact, there are a lot of things – most things – that I do not have the ability to make right. BUT! I do know the One that does! When I remember my limitations and recognize God's authority, then I can trust with full assurance that "everything is going to be all right."

Matthew 8:23-27
And when he [Jesus] was entered into a ship, his disciples followed him. And, behold, there arose a great tempest in the sea, insomuch that the ship was covered with the waves: but he was asleep. And his disciples came to *him*, and awoke him, saying, Lord, save us: we perish. And he saith unto them, Why are ye fearful, O ye of little faith? Then he arose, and rebuked the winds and the sea; and there was a great calm. But the men marvelled, saying, What manner of man is this, that even the winds and the sea obey him!

Eye Problems

And why beholdest thou the mote that is in thy brother's eye, but considerest not the beam that is in thine own eye?
-Matthew 7:3

It does surprise me at how easy it is for me to see faults in others and how easy it is to overlook my own flaws. All too often, I want to become a surgeon and remove that flaw from others before I do a little surgery on myself. I found a little poem by an unknown poet that speaks clearly to the "eye problem."

> There is so much good in the worst of us,
> And so much bad in the best of us,
> That it ill behooves any of us,
> To say anything about the rest of us.
> -Anon.

"If you judge people, you have no time to love them."
– Mother Teresa

> "How few there are who have courage enough to own their faults, or resolution enough to mend them." -Benjamin Franklin

Get to Know You

It was when our youngest daughter was going through those awkward years of turning from a child into a teenager that she uttered some profound wisdom. It happened during one of those times when Lynette was having a disagreement with her parents or parent as it was that day. The parenting rules were not fitting her desires this day, and she was extremely frustrated with me. Emotions were running high as she blurted out this statement with tears running down her cheeks: "You won't let me be me!"

I must confess that the sincerity and innocence of the statement had a very disarming effect on me; and I gave it several seconds before replying, "And who are you?"

The question had caught her totally off guard but with only a second or two of hesitation she answered, "I'm Lynette!"

A bit of wisdom that astonished me! Wasn't that what her mother and I wanted to accomplish? To train our daughter to be an independent individual who knew who she was and her place in this world.

Get to know you! Know who you are. Know your weaknesses and your strengths. Know you! Seek God's help in finding yourself because there are things about you that only He can reveal to you – but find the real you and get to know him or her well.

> *He who trims himself to suit everyone will soon whittle himself away.*
> *-Raymond Hull*

Guard My Mouth

Set a guard over my mouth, O Lord;
   Keep watch over the door of my lips
                Psalm 141:3 (NIV)

Lord, guard my mouth! If there is a single key to living happily and peacefully, this is it. I can't begin to count the number of times my big mouth has gotten me into big trouble. Words are like feathers; once let loose in the wind, it is almost impossible to gather them all back. The secret is never to let them loose.

Thus, David asks God to keep a guard over his mouth and to shut the door of his lips before un-retractable words came out. When King David of the bible penned these words, he was a man running from a relentless foe who wanted his head - literally! It would have been easy for him to say things he would later regret. He requested a guard for his mouth, a Watcher for his lips! He desired a fully functional brain that would rule his tongue.

"Nothing is more like a wise man than a fool who holds his tongue."
                                                        -Francis de Sales

"Learn to hold thy tongue; five words cost Zacharias forty weeks of silence." -Thomas Fuller

"The old country doctor of my boyhood days always began his examination by saying, 'Let me see your tongue.' It is a good way to start the examination of anybody." -Vance Havner

Honest Weights

The man had experienced the dark side of favoritism within his family. His father favored his older brother over him. In the eyes of his father, he would always be overshadowed by the first born. The wimpy little mommy's boy had no chance against his rough-and-ready big-game-hunting brother. It was easy for Dad to favor his brother.

Now a father himself, Jacob would make the same mistake preferring Joseph above his other sons. Jacob's inconsistent treatment of his children would allow the seeds of hatred to grow within his family and eventually cause him years of heartache.

Often, we wish to choose and pick the standards that we live by when dealing with those we favor. We choose another set of standards when dealing with those we dislike and yet another set of standards when dealing with ourselves. Such inconsistencies not only leave others confused but also leads to great moral confusion within our own character.

> **The Bible says:**
>
> Do not have two differing weights in your bag—one heavy, one light. Do not have two differing measures in your house—one large, one small. You must have accurate and honest weights and measures...
> -Deuteronomy 25:13 (NIV)

I wish I had…

I'm one of those fellows who never knows what to say at the time but then spends the next week thinking, I wish I'd thought to say that.
                                                –Max Lucado

I too am one of those fellows! I can't count the number of times that I have been thumped or stumped by someone and have not been able to respond in a proper manner or with the right words. Occasionally, I make things worse by uttering something foolish or allowing my temper to take charge. A few times I have had the wisdom to keep my mouth shut only to stew for days replaying the answers or responses I wish I had said.

Rehearsing the matter appears to be a waste of energy because you will never be able to relive that moment; but I have found that spending time thinking about what I should have said has its benefits. God can use those moments when you lacked the right words and had an abundance of wrong words to prepare you. Eating shoe leather because you have stuck your foot in your mouth can be a great teacher. You can rest assured there will be future events when you need to respond with the right words in the right manner.

> If any of you lack wisdom, let him ask of God, that giveth to all men liberally, and upbraideth not; and it shall be given him. -James 1:5

Leaders Lead

After a tremendous victory over Jericho, Joshua, listening to the advice of his military men, decided that the next military target, a city named Ai, was a soft target. Sending 3,000 men, Joshua would find that without the Lord's help, there are no easy targets.

It is what he did after getting things squared up with the Lord that is most interesting. The Bible says, "...but Joshua spent that night with the people ... and he and the leaders of Israel marched before them to Ai" (Joshua 8:9, 10 NIV). The troops and the people had received a mighty blow to their confidence. Joshua was a leader because he led. Leaders lead!

Leadership is not management. Leadership is leading. You do not manage people nor do you drive people in a direction like a sheepdog nipping at their heels. You lead people. This is true in every area of life. If you are a parent, you will be a better parent if you lead by example, by modeling correct behavior. The same is true for any position you may hold in life. People follow leaders and tend to dislike pushers.

Be a leader by leading.

> **Leadership:**
> *The art of getting someone else to do something you want done because he wants to do it.*
> -Dwight D. Eisenhower

Learn to Bite Your Tongue

Jonathan was a man caught between the love for his father, Saul, and love for his friend, David. He danced on a tightrope with his loyalty. Jonathan would warn David of Saul's misguided intentions but would remain at his father's side until they both would die in battle.

Perhaps one of the most interesting encounters found in the Bible is that found in the twentieth chapter of First Samuel. Saul confronts Jonathan about his friendship with David. Being driven by near insanity, Saul loses his temper when his son tries to reason with him and throws a Javelin at his son in a rage.

Jonathan is rightfully angry with his father but "bites his tongue"! Perhaps out of respect or perhaps out of fear or perhaps because Jonathan knew this proverb:

A fool shows his annoyance at once, but a prudent man overlooks an insult. –Proverbs 12:16 (NIV)

A wise person will learn that there are times to keep your mouth shut – even if you have every right to speak out. It's always easier to mend a relationship or win a disagreement when there are fewer words to bury. Learn when to bite your tongue.

> *"The best time for you to hold your tongue is the time you feel you must say something or bust"*
> *- Josh Billings*

Learn to Forgive

Never put on the face of bitterness. It will scare those around you and make you an extremely ugly person.

Bitterness stems from an unforgiving heart. Rare is the person that does not experience some injustice or some wrong that has wounded their spirit. What we do about the wrong will dictate the person we will be. We must learn to forgive.

Forgiveness is not normal – revenge is. The carnal nature demands payback – justice for injustice. Of course, this is not always possible and definitely not profitable. Therefore, we store up our perceived wrongs deep inside until they spring up as bitterness.

Learning to forgive is a process.

We are commanded by God to forgive others. Yet, forgiveness is seldom an instantaneous accomplishment. Forgiveness requires a conscious decision by the forgivers that often has to be repeated several times before it is truly realized in the heart and the mind.

Forgiveness will require God's grace.

Confess your ill feelings to God. Explain your case to God; and leave the "payback" in the hands of God. When you let go of your desire for revenge, you will be able to forgive and be released from the chains of bitterness. Count on God's grace to make it so!

Clear Up Misunderstandings Quickly

Misunderstandings between you and others will occur. Take the initiative to rectify the misunderstanding even if you believe you are in the right. The longer you let the misunderstanding go the more difficult it becomes to resolve the situation.

> Therefore if thou bring thy gift to the altar, and there rememberest that thy brother hath ought against thee; Leave there thy gift before the altar, and go thy way; first be reconciled to thy brother, and then come and offer thy gift.
> -Matthew 5:23-24

Empty Bitterness

During the course of life, I have run across more than my share of bitter people; and have on a number of occasions been faced with bitterness taking root in my own life. I have found this little thought from F. B. Meyer to be helpful.

> I have poured out my soul before the Lord.
> -1 Samuel 1:15.

> HANNAH'S soul was full of complaint and grief, which flowed over into her face and made it sorrowful. But when she had poured out her soul before the Lord, emptying out all its bitterness, the peace of God took the place of her soul-anguish, she went her way, and did eat, and her countenance was no more sad. What a glad exchange! How great the contrast! How much the better for herself, and for her home!

> Is your face darkened by the bitterness of your soul? Perhaps the enemy has been vexing you sorely; or there is an unrealized hope, an unfulfilled purpose. in your life; or, perchance, the Lord seems to have forgotten you. Poor sufferer, there is nothing for it but to pour out your soul before the Lord. Empty out its contents in confession and prayer. God knows it all; yet tell Him, as if He knew nothing. "Ye people, pour out your hearts before Him. God is a refuge for us." "In everything, by prayer and supplication make your requests known unto God."

> As we pour out our bitterness, God pours in his peace. Weeping goes out of one door whilst joy enters at another. We transmit the cup of tears to the Man of Sorrows, and He hands it back to us filled with the

blessings of the new covenant. Some day you will come to the spot where you wept and prayed, bringing your offering of praise and thanksgiving.

--from About Our Daily Homily by F. B. Meyer

"Acrid bitterness inevitably seeps into the lives of people who harbor grudges and suppress anger, and bitterness is always a poison. It keeps your pain alive instead of letting you deal with it and get beyond it. Bitterness sentences you to relive the hurt over and over."
-Lee Strobel

"Frequently the enemy entices Christians to harbor an unforgiving spirit - a very common symptom indeed among God's children. Such bitterness and fault-finding and enmity inflict a severe blow upon spiritual life." -Watchman Nee

Wisdom Snippet

"Nothing can alter the character of God. In the course of a human life, tastes and outlook and temper may change radically: a kin, equable man may turn bitter and crotchety: a man of good-will may grow cynical and callous. But nothing of this sort happens to the Creator."

-J.I. Packer

Learn to Respect

Learn to respect. Wisdom begins with a fear (i.e. an awesome respect) for the Lord. A person that wishes to engraft wisdom into her or his life must learn to reverence God at all times. By doing so, you will learn to respect yourself.

You must learn to respect you! This is not a natural process. Mark Twain said, "When people do not respect us we are sharply offended; yet in his private heart no man much respects himself." The current thinking of the world is too undercut each other - to drag someone down so that by some warped thinking we might feel better about ourselves. Learn to respect you! In doing so, you will learn to respect others.

You will know you are respecting yourself when you are respecting others. People that lack respect for parents, neighbors, teachers, and so on are lacking in personal respect for themselves.

"If you want to be respected, you must respect yourself."
-Spanish Proverb

> *"Every human being, of whatever origin, of whatever station, deserves respect. We must each respect others even as we respect ourselves*
> *-Ulysses S. Grant*

Learn to Love Yourself

Unless you learn to love you, you will have a difficult time fulfilling Jesus' command, "Thou shalt love thy neighbour as thyself." (Romans 13:9)

Love cannot exist without respect. This is true when applied to loving others and also true when learning to love yourself.

Learn to respect yourself by clearing your conscience before God. Like the Prodigal Son, your heavenly Father will accept you not as a mere servant but as a cherished son. If God, the creator of the universe deems you a cherished son, then you should see yourself as an ambassador for the King of Kings. First respect you and then love you!

There is a difference between being "in love" with yourself, which is pride and vain, and loving yourself. Make sure you know the difference.

The same definition found in 1 Corinthians 13:4-7 for loving others also applies for loving yourself.

> Love is patient, love is kind. It does not envy, it does not boast, it is not proud. It is not rude, it is not self-seeking, it is not easily angered, it keeps no record of wrongs. Love does not delight in evil but rejoices with the truth. It always protects, always trusts, always hopes, always perseveres. (NIV)

A real love for you will always strive to build up and never tear down. If you have a healthy love of self, then your choices are for the good.

Accept God's Forgiveness

If God forgives us, we must forgive ourselves otherwise its like setting up ourselves as a higher tribunal than Him.

-C. S. Lewis

From today and every day that follows learn to accept God's forgiveness. Do not be counted among that great number of people that never learn to forgive themselves. If you have truly sought God's forgiveness, then God has forgiven you! Now, today, forgive yourself and get on with your life.

If we confess our sins, he is faithful and just to forgive us our sins, and to cleanse us from all unrighteousness. -1 John 1:9

Wisdom Snippet

Love yourself and also like yourself!

It will be difficult for others to like you if you do not like you. Build on those qualities that you like about yourself and change those qualities that can cause you to dislike yourself.

Learn When To Say No!

The scene was grim and the faces of all those gathered there were long and sad. The muffled sob of an elderly lady echoed the sorrow that overshadowed the task ahead. A retired lifelong farmer and his loving wife of fifty years were being evicted from their home and their farm. The creditors had foreclosed and the farm that had been in the family for three generations would be auctioned off.

The farmer's eldest son, along with his younger brother, had approached Dad with a need. The new construction business they had started was about to boom. They had landed a large contract with a fast expanding retail business that would net them big dollars. All they needed was a little capital. The bank needed a little more surety. Would Dad co-sign for a loan?

Hesitating for only a moment, the loving father would choose to back his two sons. After all, they were good boys with a strong knowledge of construction and history of hard work.

Both boys worked hard and put in long hours. They kept their end of the bargain. All looked well until the super growing retail business failed. Then the nightmare began and lasted for months until this day.

> *The eyes of love and the desire to succeed had hidden three biblical principles:*
>
> - **Never co-sign for a loan!**
> - **You have no guarantee of tomorrow!**
> - **Learn to Say No!**

1. Never co-sign for a loan!

Don't guarantee to pay someone else's debt. If you don't have the money, you might lose your bed.

Proverbs 22:26-27 (CEV)

This is really a straight-forward nugget of wisdom from the Bible that says exactly what is said; but it is one piece of wisdom that many choose to ignore. What are we to say when that friend who really needs a car to go to work asks you to cosign for the payments? What are we to tell that church member that needs a cosigner? What are we to tell that adult child that wishes to buy that first home – but needs a cosigner? It is often hard to say no but when it comes to this issue – no is the biblical and wise answer.

2. You have no guarantee of tomorrow!

Now listen, you who say, "Today or tomorrow we will go to this or that city, spend a year there, carry on business and make money." Why, you do not even know what will happen tomorrow.

James 4:13-14a (NIV)

Here is a simple explanation why you should never cosign for a loan. God knows, and you should too, that you have no control over another person's affairs or actions. Nor do you know what future God has in store for that individual. If their finances head south for any reason, you have no control over it. However, your life, and even more important, your relationship with that person will be deeply affected due to their misfortune or mistakes. You will no longer be able to support and pray for them like you should.

Continued

Jesus gave us a little insight into dealing with these situations. He said, "lend, hoping for nothing again" (Luke 6:35). If you have it and can give it without needing it to be returned (Note: the word "give"), then do so. If you can't then don't!

3. Learn to Say No!

Simply let your 'Yes' be 'Yes,' and your 'No,' 'No'; anything beyond this comes from the evil one.
-Matthew 5:37 (NIV)

It is good to remember that we are not always helping people by saying yes. If you are afraid that by telling the person "no" you'll lose their relationship, just remember that by telling them yes, you might run the same risk.

> *Intense feeling too often obscures the truth.* -Harry S. Truman

Let's Decorate the Tree or Maybe Not!

Among the most amusing memories of Christmases past are those when our family went searching for the prefect Christmas tree. When I was young, back shortly after the Mayflower docked at Plymouth, the artificial tree had not been invented and the prefect living evergreen tree was difficult to discover.

A few days before Christmas we would begin searching the Christmas tree lots for the perfect pine tree; the tree that looked exactly like the one on the cover of *Life Magazine*. This shopping adventure could have taken hours had not the cold weather and the beckoning of hot chocolate brought about a compromise. Of course, we never found a prefect tree!

The real adventure began when we attempted to make our imperfect tree, which leaned to the left and had several obvious bare spots, into the prefect tree. Lights, tinsel, and homemade decorations, including strung popcorn, were properly placed on the tree until the tree itself could barely be seen.

Christmas, the celebration of the birth of the Messiah, is approached the same way. We decorate Christmas with tinsel and lights until the real meaning is lost to dinner parties and gifts; and the real story of Christmas is lost in major television and movie productions of Santa and his elves. Often forgotten is the purpose of Christ's birth.

The purpose of God the Son coming into the world was to "save his people from their sins" (Matthew 1:21). Jesus did not leave heaven and take on flesh, so we could decorate a pine tree. The real Christmas story only begins at the cradle. It continues to the cross, and climaxes with an empty cave.

Christmas is about God's love and His desire to redeem his people from their sins. The purpose of Christ coming must not be lost in the glitter of Christmas trees, gifts, and jolly old men in red suits.

Lions and Tigers! O My!

North of where we live, out in the middle of nowhere, an unusual animal shelter houses over two-hundred big cats. It is the Exotic Feline Rescue Center of Indiana and the home for lions, tigers, cougars, bobcats, and a few other exotic cats that have been rescued from negligent and sometimes abusive owners. Many of these owners have been private citizens who found that the cute little lion cub they brought home turned into a full-grown lion craving 35 pounds of meat daily and demanding a lot more room than their living room. A few have discovered the reason why they are called wild animals.

Most of these animals carry some marks from their mistreatment. Some are blind from malnutrition others have more evident physical marks. All share one thing in common. They cannot return to the wild where they long to be because they would not survive; but they also are not domesticated house pets.

You cannot help but wonder - what were those people thinking when they spent their good money and brought home a wild animal? Did they think it was cute? Did they think owning a lion would make them unique or outstanding? Were they on some kind of a power trip and thought having a tiger on a leash made them tough? Who knows? Nevertheless, the little striped kitty they loved became a wild animal they learned to hate.

Which brings to mind another question, why do people allow a little sin to make its home in their heart? Why does the wife or husband allow a little flirtation at work or on the Internet? Didn't they know it could turn into adultery and destroy his or her home?

Continued

Every day Christians allow a little sin, a cute cuddly little sin, have a foothold in their life only to find sin demands more and grows wild. Gambling, alcoholism, adultery, stealing, and even murder begins with a small seed of sin.

The message is simple – don't allow a little sin into your life because it always grows up. A cute little tiger cub grows into a full-size tiger and might have you for lunch!

Neither give place to the devil. (Ephesians 4:27)

Be sober, be vigilant; because your adversary the devil, as a roaring lion, walketh about, seeking whom he may devour: (1Peter 5:8)

Dance with Grandma

Dance with your grandma. It will make her day and yours. No music is required. In fact grandma does not need to be present. Dance with her anyway. Remembering your heritage and embracing the joy of it will make any day better. Try it and see.

A house needs a grandma in it.
                                    -Louisa May Alcott

The lines are fallen unto me in pleasant places; yea, I have a goodly heritage. -Psalm 16:6

Don't give into temptation – not even a little!

Flee also youthful lusts: but follow righteousness, faith, charity, peace, with them that call on the Lord out of a pure heart.
-2 Timothy 2:22

"If you yield to Satan in the least, he will carry you further and further, till he has left you under a stupefied or terrified conscience: stupefied, till thou hast lost all thy tenderness. A stone at the top of a hill, when it begins to roll down, ceases not till it comes to the bottom. Thou thinkest it is but yielding a little, and so by degrees are carried on, till thou hast sinned away all thy profession, and all principles of conscience, by the secret witchery of his temptations."
— Thomas Manton

Live a Disciplined Life

He was a young man with great potential; and for that reason the conquerors that had over ran his homeland had carried him off to their capital. He was to become part of the "brain-trust" in a faraway land for a ruthless king.

We have no record of what was going through Daniel's mind at this time; but we do have a record, of how he lived his life after arriving in Babylon. From the Bible, we can see that Daniel led an extremely disciplined life. Because of his Jewish faith, Daniel was required to follow a strict diet. He was willing to risk his life to obey God's law. He had a regular routine of praying three times a day; and his determination to observe his prayer routine would cause him to be thrown into a den full of hungry lions.

Daniel lived a disciplined life. He was consistent in his walk with God and was blessed by God despite his captivity.

Steven Covey claims in his classic bestseller, *The 7 Habits of Highly Effective People*, that effective people are proactive. They don't just sit around waiting for things to happen but make them happen. Because most people are not disciplined, they are always waiting for something to happen to them or for them.

Disciplined people make things happen. They pay the price and get the education they need to succeed. They save the money and go without so they can take their dream trip. Proactive people write the books, produce the movies, and achieve their goals and dreams because they have chosen a disciplined life.

"Happiness can be defined, in part at least, as the fruit of the desire and ability to sacrifice what we want now for what we want eventually." -- Stephen Covey

But Daniel purposed in his heart... Daniel 1:8

Choose and Pay

Life is made up of a series of choices and a willingness to pay the price. If you choose to be a rocket scientist, then you must pay the price of spending the time to become a rocket scientist. Weigh the choices before you and be prepared to pay the price.

Two little notes must be added to this:
1. *Most choices do not have shortcuts around the price and*
2. *God's will should always be sought first.*

For which of you, intending to build a tower, sitteth not down first, and counteth the cost, whether he have sufficient to finish it? -Luke 14:28

Lord! Light My Candle

For thou wilt light my candle: the LORD my God will enlighten my darkness. - Psalms 18:28

Be positive and not negative! The world needs a breath of fresh hope and not the smoke of impending doom!

Get two preachers together for very long and if they are not careful, the conversations will lead to what a dark state the world has descended into. Indeed, it does appear that chaos and immorality seems to rule both the night and the day. Even so, the ministry of the saints is not to complain about how bad things are. The ministry of the saints is to be a light in a dark world. The Apostle Paul put it like this:

> Do all things without murmurings and disputings: That ye may be blameless and harmless, the sons of God, without rebuke, in the midst of a crooked and perverse nation, among whom ye shine as lights in the world; Holding forth the word of life; that I may rejoice in the day of Christ, that I have not run in vain, neither laboured in vain. - Philippians 2:14-16

May our song be that of the Psalmist – Lord make us shine as a light in darkness.

More Work Please

Serve the LORD with gladness… - Psalms 100:2

The wife and I went to dinner last night and were pleasantly surprised by the excellent service we received. The young lady who attended to us did so in a timely manner and with a positive attitude, even though we had made several requests. At one point, she checked on us asking if there was anything she could do. We replied that we were just fine and then she said something that rung my spiritual bell. She said with a smile, "You folks are just making it too easy for me. You need to start ordering me around."

Wow! What a positive attitude for service!

Can you remember telling God that He was making it too easy for you, and that He needed to start sending you MORE work? Most of the time, we are complaining about how big the load is and how difficult it is. Perhaps, it is time for an attitude adjustment.

And that little girl who served us – she got a hefty tip for her service from a tightwad like me. Can you imagine how God would reward us if we asked for more work and not less?

Never Give Up

It is said that Thomas Edison tried 10,000 times to invent the light bulb. When asked about his failures Edison replied, "I have not failed; I've just found 10,000 ways that won't work."

When Henry Ford decided he was going to produce a V8 engine, the experts were already convinced it couldn't be done. Ford set out to gather "a lot of men who have an infinite capacity to not know what can't be done." Finding a select group of engineers, Ford instructed them to do the impossible. Working on the ideas and inspiration of others who had failed, what was impossible became possible.

Jesus taught his disciples "...they should always pray and not give up." (Luke 18:1 NIV)

Most of us give up too easily. We never put our heart into our efforts or our prayers. We view failures as an end and not an opportunity. History is full of unnamed people who gave up.

Never give up!

"*Many of life's failures are people who did not realize how close they were to success when they gave up.*" -Thomas Edison

> *When your dreams turn to dust, vacuum. -Author Unknown*

Failures

People who end up accomplishing much often experience failures. They make mistakes and have setbacks. But! They always fall foreword.

Thomas Edison said this about President Wilson, "*They say President Wilson has blundered. Perhaps he has, but I notice he usually blunders forward.*" Learn from your mistakes and press forward.

I press toward the mark for the prize of the high calling of God in Christ Jesus.
 —Philippians 3:14

Personalize the Promise

> The promises of the Bible should be made personal. They take root in our lives when we engraft them into our heart, mind, and life.

When God had promised her the desire of her heart, she found it difficult to believe that he could keep his promise. As the years passed by and the promise continued to go unanswered, she tried to reason that the promise was an impossibility, and if it was to be fulfilled, she would need to take things into her hands. That proved to be a mistake.

Then God renewed his promise. This time, however, God made it so that the promise would become personal. Sarai would get a new name, a slightly different name. She now would be called Sarah. God personalized her promise.

The promises of the Bible should be made personal. They take root in our lives when we engraft them into our heart, mind, and life. The promises are meant to be realized within the soul of the believer.

A great Bible promise is:

> And we know that all things work together for good to them that love God, to them who are the called according to his purpose.
> - Romans 8:28

For this promise to become real in our life, we must replace the word "them" with our own name. We must become the one that loves God. We must believe we are called to a divine purpose. And, we must internalize the promise that everything works for our good.

View this promise as personal. Read it and engraft it into your life. It should read like this:

> And [your name] knows that all things work together for good of [your name] who loves God, who is the called according to his purpose. (The personalization of - Romans 8:28)

When you learn to personalize God's promises, the power of God will radically change your life.

The promises of God to those that love Him are many. Following are a few that you can easily personalize.

HIS PRESENCE WITH US

"Fear thou not; for I am with thee" (Isaiah 41:10).
(Example: "Fear not [your name]; for I am with you [your name])

"The LORD is with you, while ye be with him; and if ye seek him, he will be found of you" (2Chronicles 15:2).

"The LORD, he it is that doth go before thee; he will be with thee, he will not fail thee, neither forsake thee" (Deuteronomy 31:8).

HIS LOVE

"He will love thee, and bless thee, and multiply thee" (Deuteronomy 7:13).

"I have loved thee with an everlasting love: therefore with lovingkindness have I drawn thee" (Jeremiah 31:3).

"For the Father himself loveth you, because ye have loved me" (John 16:27).

HIS MERCY

"Like as a father pitieth his children, so the LORD pitieth them that fear him. The mercy of the LORD is from everlasting to everlasting upon them that fear him" (Psalm 103:13, 17).

HIS HELP

"If God be for us, who can be against us?" (Romans 8:31).

"We may boldly say, The Lord is my helper, and I will not fear what man shall do unto me" (Hebrews 13:6).

"I will strengthen thee; yea, I will help thee; yea, I will uphold thee with the right hand of my righteousness. I the LORD thy God will hold thy right hand, saying unto thee, Fear not; I will help thee. Fear not, thou worm Jacob, and ye men of Israel; I will help thee, saith the LORD, and thy redeemer, the Holy One of Israel" (Isaiah 41:10, 13, 14).

HIS CARE

"There shall not an hair of your head perish" (Luke 21:18).

"The very hairs of your head are all numbered" (Matthew 10:30).

Source: Samuel Clarke, D.D., PRECIOUS BIBLE PROMISES, 1750

Develop an Eye

May we suggest that you begin developing an eye for God's promise by keeping a journal of all the promises you find while reading through the Bible.

The Square

Some of my favorite childhood memories are walking around the town square of a small town in the southern part of Illinois. At that time, the "square" was the center of commerce. The square was where the two "Dime Stores" (i.e. variety store) were located, and they came complete with hands-on-toys that you could play with even if you didn't buy them. The square hosted a drugstore with a soda fountain that served Cherry Cokes for one dime. And the square also was home to the only movie house where one thin quarter would get you a double feature and keep you out of Mom's hair all afternoon.

Smack in the middle of the square was the only building that didn't sell anything – the county court house. There they dished out justice sometimes at bargain prices and other times at an extremely costly price. Fortunately, most of my friends and I managed to avoid the long arm of the law; and therefore, we avoided the courthouse and its justice.

According to Easton's Revised Bible Dictionary, justice "is rendering to everyone that which is his due. It has been distinguished from equity in this respect, that while justice means merely the doing what positive law demands, equity means the doing of what is fair and right in every separate case."

Real justice is served when we get what we deserve; and in the "deserving account," we are lacking. We really do not want justice. We want mercy!

"The difference between mercy and grace? Mercy gave the prodigal son a second chance. Grace gave him a feast." -Max Lucado

Prudence

A thesaurus would give you several words related to prudence. Cautiousness, discretion, and good sense are among the words used. Good sense, which is sometimes referred to as common sense, is a good way to describe prudence. The Bible tells us that wisdom and prudence or common sense, dwell together (Proverbs 8:12). Where you find the one, you will also find the other.

Practice good sense and you will be viewed by others as a wise man.

Good sense is a thing all need, few have, and none think they want.
-Benjamin Franklin

Read

He was somewhat embarrassed of his uneducated father. He, himself, never had the opportunity of a formal education. However, he would rise to hold the respect, of not only his peers, but of thousands of future people that would read about him. The honor for earning such respect is rooted in the fact that he had an unquenchable thirst for reading.

Abraham Lincoln, the lanky, unattractive, backwoodsman, would lead his nation in one of the most difficult times in its history. The man who was always concerned about his lack of education would prove to be brilliant. How could this be? Because he read! **Again, I say read!**

Read through the Bible yearly.

There is no greater moral compass for life than the Bible. The Bible teaches that the beginning of wisdom and of understanding starts with a reverence for God. Every possible subject and life lesson is addressed within the pages of the Bible. Know it and you will know God.

Read biographies of noble people.

You will gain from their wisdom and learn from their life. By reading of the lives of others, you will be able to understand your place in the world. You will find encouragement and challenges that will drive you to excel. You will also find hope. Yes, an abused boy deaf in one ear can become a Thomas Edison, and a couple of bicycle mechanics can build a flying machine.

Read what interests you!

It is those areas of life that hold your interest that often becomes the area you find the most satisfying. They also become the areas that define you.

Don't live your life through fiction.

Reading for entertainment is enjoyable but be careful! Life is not found in a fiction book. Life is living it!

Today a reader, tomorrow a leader. -Margaret Fuller

Woodpecker Wisdom

Wherefore they are no more twain, but one flesh. What therefore God hath joined together, let not man put asunder.
- Matthew 19:6

Solomon, even when he was walking close with the Lord and had great wisdom, didn't have the commonsense wisdom of a woodpecker. The same wisdom Solomon was lacking is lacking in a lot of people today. What is the common sense wisdom that woodpeckers have and many people don't? Many species of woodpeckers mate for life – the same mate for their entire life!

In our throwaway culture today, people change mates almost as often as they change cars, leaving in the wake a lot of confused children while carrying a load of baggage into a new relationship. The result is children who have difficultly bonding in relationships because they have no model to follow and the destruction of the family unit.

Most woodpeckers have more sense. We should too!

> **Before you marry…**
>
> *"If you are a child of God and you marry a child of the Devil, you're going to have trouble with your father-in-law."* --Max Lucado

Relationships

Develop a lasting relationship with God and with others. Spend the time and effort to build good personal relationships with others. These close relationships will become your anchors through life's storms.

A growing personal relationship between your spouse, your children, your family, and your friends are priorities. The order of importance is as follows: God is first. Your spouse, if you are married, is always next. Your children followed by your family are next in line of importance. Your friends follow family. Do not underestimate their importance.

Relationships require time. There is no substitute for time. Quality time, although important, will never take the place of quantity.

For relationships to survive and thrive, they must be approached with a spirit of forgiveness and an understanding heart.

> **A Prayer**
>
> *Help me to love what is important and not to love what the world loves. Help me to love my family, my brothers and sisters in Christ, and you with the kind of love you have for me. Help me to learn to also love my enemies. Amen.*
>
> *And the Lord direct your hearts into the love of God, and into the patient waiting for Christ. 2Th 3:5)*

Self-Worth

The Bible instructs us "not to think *of himself* more highly than he ought to think; but to think soberly, according as God hath dealt to every man the measure of faith" (Romans 12:3). While we must always be conscious of the pride factor, we must not enter a false humility that is really cloaked pride. We must "think soberly, according as God hath dealt to every man."

Each of us have our weak points, but we also have our strong points. It is these strong points where we need to build our sense of worth. Each person has been put on planet earth for a reason, and it is to develop and exercise those strong points for the glory of God.

Find your self-worth in the love of the Lord. You are so important in the heart and eyes of God that his only Son, Jesus, died for you. **You are that important!**

"Many of us harbor hidden low self-esteem. We deem everything and everyone more important that ourselves and think that meeting their needs is more important than meeting our own. But if you run out of gas, everyone riding with you will be left stranded." -T.D. Jakes

"Sin is believing the lie that you are self-created, self-dependent and self-sustained." –Augustine

But ye are a chosen generation, a royal priesthood, an holy nation, a peculiar people; that ye should shew forth the praises of him who hath called you out of darkness into his marvellous light: -1 Peter 2:9

Speak Encouragement

Many that you will meet today will have a heavy heart. They will be weighted down by any number of cares and concerns. The devil never misses an opportunity to dump on a heavy heart.

Today, decide to speak words of encouragement and hope to those that you meet. By doing so, you will not only help a weighty heart stand tall; you will also lighten the weight on your own heart. Walk upright in the footsteps of our Lord Jesus Christ. Choose today to follow God's grace and practice the following principle:

Heaviness in the heart of man maketh it stoop: but a good word maketh it glad. - Proverbs 12:25

> **The Church...**
>
> The local church assembles not only to worship God and learn more about him but also to encourage each other.
>
> *Let us not give up meeting together, as some are in the habit of doing, but let us encourage one another — and all the more as you see the Day approaching.*
> *Hebrews 10:25*

Seek to be Meek!

Meekness is strength under control.

Albert Barnes defines meekness as "patience in the reception of injuries. It is neither meanness, nor a surrender of our rights, nor cowardice; but it is the opposite of sudden anger, of malice, of long-harbored vengeance."

We practice meekness when we quietly endure injustices for the sake of Christ or when we hold our tongue when we have the right to explode. It is a quality that requires the work of the Holy Spirit within us and cannot truly be produced by our own efforts.

Meekness is also a characteristic of a mature believer.

The practice of meekness is especially beneficial in relationships and in leadership. Seek to be meek.

> He that hath no rule over his own spirit is like
> a city that is broken down, and without walls.
> 								-Proverbs 25:28

Thank You Lord for Your Patience

Forty years long was I grieved with *this* generation, and said, It *is* a people that do err in their heart, and they have not known my ways: - Psalms 95:10

Have you considered how patient the Lord is? For forty years after miraculously delivering Israel from captivity, the Lord was still waiting for the people to trust him. Despite his generosity of feeding them manna from heaven and allowing them to drink from the rock, they were a faithless people that often rebelled and sinned. Nevertheless, they remained his people.

Many today have traveled the same path. Even though they have been delivered from the penalty of sin by the blood of Jesus, many believers continue to be wayward saints. They never grasp the full joy of their salvation nor have they found freedom from their sin. Their faith has been lacking and their loyalty even less. However, God continues to be faithful. God remains patient.

Have you considered the Lord's patience? Is God patiently waiting for you? Where would you be had not God been patient with you?

But thou, O Lord, art a God full of compassion, and gracious, longsuffering, and plenteous in mercy and truth. Psalms 86:15

The Lord is not slack concerning his promise, as some men count slackness; but is longsuffering to us-ward, not willing that any should perish, but that all should come to repentance. 2 Peter 3:9

The Blessings of Having Little

When Solomon was a young man, he was suddenly thrust into ruling a Kingdom. Solomon felt inadequate and unworthy of ruling such a large Kingdom. Therefore, he sought wisdom from the Lord. He would rely on the Lord for guidance.

Later in life, when he and the Kingdom prospered; Solomon's feeling of inadequacy was replaced with pride; and his reliance on God was replaced with a harem of trophy wives. The cost of doing so was high. Solomon's beloved Kingdom would be divided as would his family.

Most of us do not look at having less as a blessing; but it could well be so. The Lord warned Israel about the dangers of prosperity saying:

> Lest when thou hast eaten and art full, and hast built goodly houses, and dwelt therein; And when thy herds and thy flocks multiply, and thy silver and thy gold is multiplied, and all that thou hast is multiplied; Then thine heart be lifted up, and thou forget the LORD thy God, which brought thee forth out of the land of Egypt, from the house of bondage; - Deuteronomy 8:12-14

Prosperity can cause you to forget your love for the Lord. The Lord warned the prosperous Church of Ephesus about losing her first love – the love for the Lord.

Prosperity can do more than cause you to forget your love for the Lord; it can also cause you to fall in love with the world. CS Lewis addressed this issue in his book the *Screwtape Letters* when a demon makes these observations about mankind:

> "Prosperity knits a man to the World. He feels that he is 'finding his place in it', while really it is finding its place in him. His increasing reputation, his widening circle of acquaintances, his sense of importance, the growing pressure of absorbing and agreeable work, build up in him a sense of being really at home in earth which is just what we want."

Perhaps the real blessings – the hidden blessings – are those blessings of having not.

Remove far from me vanity and lies: give me neither poverty nor riches; feed me with food convenient for me: Lest I be full, and deny thee, and say, Who is the LORD? or lest I be poor, and steal, and take the name of my God in vain. Psalms 30:8-9

"We must accept finite disappointment, but we must never lose infinite hope." -Martin Luther King

Abandon

Abandon your will to the will of the Lord. Contentment and peace will be difficult to find as long as you are resolved to have your way. There is a path that God has for you. It is narrow and may be difficult at times but in the long run it is always best.

Follow the example of the Lord Jesus: "For I came down from heaven, not to do mine own will, but the will of him that sent me." *-John 6:38*

The Homeless Child, Jesus

But when Jesus saw it, he was much displeased, and said unto them, Suffer the little children to come unto me, and forbid them not: for of such is the kingdom of God. (Mark 10:14)

My wife's work with the School District allows her to minister to many homeless children. When she asked me to help with a Christmas party at the local homeless shelter, I was a little hesitant; but being the faithful husband, I tagged along. I'm glad I did!

It was a humble reminder that in "the land of plenty" there are plenty of people – children who have found "no room in the inn." Over fifty, children crowded around my feet to listen to the Christmas Story. Some of these children were there because of the poor choices of their parents. Others were there because of unforeseen circumstances – but not one child was there due to their own fault.

A Prayer: The Heart of Jesus

Love and compassion is the heart of Jesus, as demonstrated on the cross. Lord I wish to have a compassionate heart. Let my treatment of others be as kind as you have treated me. Amen.

The Meaning of Life

"Meaningless! Meaningless!" says the Teacher. "Utterly meaningless! Everything is meaningless."

- Ecclesiastes 1:2 (NIV)

Solomon's hair was turning gray when he wrote Ecclesiastes. He had lived a full life, a rich life, a powerful life, a wise life, and a foolish life. Even so, like many people, he began to look for meaning, for the purpose to the scheme of it all. He had difficulty finding any meaning and making any sense out of life as long as he searched horizontally. While viewing life on an earthly, physical plane it seemed to be an endless loop that always ended in death.

Solomon's conclusion was that the only true meaning to life; the only true purpose in life was not to be found by looking horizontally but by looking vertically. Only in God and in obedience to His will can the real meaning and purpose to life be found. Solomon ended his book with this final statement:

> Let us hear the conclusion of the whole matter: Fear God, and keep his commandments: for this *is* the whole *duty* of man. For God shall bring every work into judgment, with every secret thing, whether *it be* good, or whether *it be* evil. (Ecclesiastes 12:13-14)

Wise words! May we learn from them!

Man's chief end is to glorify God, and to enjoy him forever.
WESTMINSTER SHORTER CATECHISM

The Pursuit of ~~Happiness~~ Holiness

The famed Declaration of Independence contains this legendary quotation: "We hold these truths to be self-evident, that all men are created equal, that they are endowed by their Creator with certain unalienable Rights, that among these are Life, Liberty and the pursuit of Happiness."

Way before the Declaration of Independence, people have been trying to pursue happiness only to fail. Why? Because happiness cannot be found outside of holiness!

Several centuries earlier, Israel's King David wrote: "Depart from evil, and do good; seek peace, and pursue it" (Psalms 34:14). This simple verse, although not as well-known as the famous quotation in the Declaration of Independence, contains a summary of how holiness; and thus happiness can be obtained. The three pillars of holiness that lead to happiness are:

- **Depart (i.e. leave, flee) evil.**
- **Do good.**
- **Pursue peace.**

All three share the common thought that action must be taken – depart, do, pursue are all action words. Holiness is to be sought after. Holiness does not just happen. It is pursued and pursued vigorously.

While it is proper to ask God not to lead us into temptations and to deliver us from evil, it is also proper for God to require of us to take the action that removes us from temptation!

When Potiphar's wife tried to seduce Joseph, Joseph fled from her (Check out Genesis 39). Real happiness can only be found when you are earnestly and vigorously departing from evil.

God requires us to do more than just avoid evil. He expects us to DO GOOD! The Bible teaches that every born-again believer was ordained to do good; and not to do good is a sin!

> For we are his workmanship, created in Christ Jesus unto good works, which God hath before ordained that we should walk in them. Ephesians 2:10

> Therefore to him that knoweth to do good, and doeth it not, to him it is sin. (James 4:17)

Departing from evil and doing good will greatly help you in your quest of holiness; but God also expects us to pursue peace! It's this last pillar of holiness that is often missing.

Many "prune faced" church goers are missing the joy of their salvation because they have forgotten to pursue peace.

Often, some of the "holiest church workers" can be some of the most cantankerous, difficult, and unhappy people ever to grace planet earth. While they follow the strictest obedience and labor at being "do-gooders", they remain on the constant prowl for a good fight! They work at putting their "gift" of criticism and strife into action. They are to be pitied and prayed for because they are missing an important link to finding the joy of their faith. They do not seek peace. Don't be counted among them.

Be Alert

Keep watch! Be alert. The devil never sleeps. As a child of God, your testimony is extremely important. The devil will try to trick you into either calling evil good or good evil. He will try to deceive you into rationalizing away sin. Trust the Bible to lead you correctly and keep a good testimony.

Be sober, be vigilant; because your adversary the devil, as a roaring lion, walketh about, seeking whom he may devour:
-1 Peter 5:8

The Past

Are you a Mall Watcher? Are you one of those people who are dragged to the mall usually by a spouse? And the only thing that keeps you from going bonkers are the benches near the hub where you can sit and watch the people go by? That's me. I am a member in good standing with the Mall Watchers.

What I enjoy most is observing the dress, style, and actions of people and trying to identify what time period they are stuck in. Some are easy to spot like the older lady with the poodle skirt and gray hair in a pony tail – the fifties! My favorite is the senior hippie with the long hair, bell-bottom pants, and a headband with "peace signs" imprinted in the design. Now there is a guy who wants to resurrect the seventies.

Some people get stuck in the past. They live their life either wanting to resurrect the past or haunted by the past. Are you one of those stuck in the past?

The "Past" can either be a hindrance where you remain stuck and are robbed of the joy of the "Now" and the hope of the "Future"; or on the other hand, it can be a motivator that pushes you to excellence. The past can become your teacher or your slave master. The choice is yours.

> Brethren, I count not myself to have apprehended: but [this] one thing [I do], forgetting those things which are behind, and reaching forth unto those things which are before, I press toward the mark for the prize of the high calling of God in Christ Jesus. –Philippians 3:13-14

This is the Year the Lord has Given Us

> This is the day which the LORD hath made; we will rejoice and be glad in it.
> - Psalms 118:24

One day the sun was shinning brightly, and the optimist said, "Great day, eh?"

The pessimist said, "The stupid sun will burn the crops."

The next day it rained. Again, the optimist tried to engage his friend, but the pessimist's only response was: "Stinking rain will wash out all the seed!"

So the optimist took his friend duck hunting, which he loved. After the first duck was shot the optimist dispatched his dog to fetch the duck. The dog ran on top of the water, picked up the duck and ran back.

The optimist exclaimed, "Did you see that?"

The pessimist replied, "Dog can't swim, eh?"

The point is simple. The way you view the coming day or the coming year depends upon your attitude – both the mental and the spiritual attitude. You may choose to approach the day with great anticipation and excitement, or you may choose to approach the new day with dread and defeat. The choice is yours!

A pessimist is one who makes difficulties of his opportunities, and an optimist is one who makes opportunities of his difficulties.
-Harry S. Truman

Time to Put the Brakes On!

Stephen Leacock once wrote: "How strange is our little procession called life! The child says, 'When I am big...' and then, grown up, he or she says, 'When I am married.' But then the thought turns to 'When I am able to retire.' Then when retirement comes, we look back over the landscape traversed. A cold wind blows over it. Somehow we have missed it all, and it is gone. Life, we learn too late, is in the living, in the tissue of every day and hour."

All too often, we find ourselves *running* through the day with very few pauses to enjoy the day. We eat too fast and the flavor of food is lost. Our eyes never stop long enough to see the entire beauty of a morning sky. We fail to cuddle the gentle touch of a child. We do not embrace a sweet kiss from our spouse. We do spend too much time worrying about tomorrow and trying to fix yesterday. Our life-dial is turned to super speed; and we allow the days and years to go by without really living life. What a waste!

God, by your grace, allow us to put on the brakes. Let us see, touch, and feel the joy of today.

At the close of life the question will be not, how much you have got, but how much you have given; not how much you have won, but how much you have done; not how much you have saved, but how much you have sacrificed; how much you have loved and served, not how much you were honored.

-Nathan C. Schaeffe

Victory

Is the Devil beating you up? Do you feel like you are always losing and never winning? The answer to your problem may be as easy as turning around. Instead of running from the Devil and the problem, perhaps you should turn around and attack the problem. The book of James says, "Submit yourselves therefore to God. Resist the devil, and he will flee from you" (James 4:7). You will never find victory as long as you are retreating.

Max Lucado gives this advise:

> *Rush your giant with a God-saturated soul. Giant of divorce, you aren't entering my home! Giant of depression? It may take a lifetime, but you won't conquer me. Giant of alcohol, bigotry, child abuse, insecurity . . . you're going down. How long since you loaded your sling and took a swing at your giant?* -Max Lucado, *Facing Your Gaints*

Perhaps, it's time to lock-n-load your sling and put the Devil on the run.

The Question of Sin

C. I. Scofield reminds us of sobering facts concerning personal responsibility, sin, and the Holy Spirit.

"No Christian needs to sin. If he yields to solicitation from without, or the more subtle suggestions from within, it is because he deliberately or carelessly wills it so. The Spirit is there to break the power of sin." -C. I. Scofield

Not By Chance

When we think upon the cross and the crucifixion of our Lord Jesus, we need to remember that his death on the cross was not an accident, a fluke, but a sovereign plan foretold hundreds of years earlier in prophesy. Arthur W. Pink said:

> "Every important detail of the great tragedy had been written down beforehand. The betrayal by a familiar friend (Ps. 4 1:9), the forsaking of the disciples through being offended at him (Ps. 31:11), the false accusation (Ps. 35:11), the silence before his judges (Isa. 53:7), the being proven guiltless (Isa. 53:9), the numbering of him with transgressors (Isa. 53:12), the being crucified (Ps. 22:16), the mockery of the spectators (Ps. 109:25), the taunt of non-deliverance (Ps. 22:7, 8), the gambling for his garments (Ps. 22:18), the prayer for his enemies (Isa. 53:12), the being forsaken of God (Ps. 22:1), the thirsting (Ps. 69:2 1), the yielding of his spirit into the hands of the Father (Ps. 3 1:5), the bones not broken (Ps. 34:20), the burial in a rich man's tomb (Isa. 53:9); all plainly foretold centuries before they came to pass. What a convincing evidence of the divine inspiration of the scriptures! How firm a foundation ye saints of the Lord, is laid for your faith in his excellent word!"

It wasn't by chance that our Lord died as he did but by divine purpose. He died for you and me! Such truth should humble us.

A Whack on the Side of the Head

Roger von Oech made a great observation in his book *A Whack on the Side of the Head: How You Can Be More Creative*. We are often taught never to be foolish and tend to "go with the crowd." He says, "When everyone is thinking alike, no one is doing much thinking."

The Bible teaches us not to think as the world thinks "but be ye transformed by the renewing of your mind" (Romans 8:2). The word "renewing" means a complete renovation of our thinking process. A renovation is not the destruction of all you have learned. A renovation is a dismantling of what you have been taught and a new reconstruction of our thinking process. A renewed mind is a complete overhaul of our thinking and a realignment of life's knowledge for the better. "Therefore if any man be in Christ, he is a new creature: old things are passed away; behold, all things are become new" (2 Corinthians 5:17).

The Christian doesn't see things as the world sees things nor does he or she think like the world. The Christian doesn't "go with the crowd." He thinks in a different realm. His mind is on things above and not on things on the earth (Colossians 3:2).

Unfortunately, a few Christians need a "whack on the side of the head" and need to start thinking with a renewed mind.

Beware of stinky thinking!

Satan wants your mind to run on the road of sin and hopelessness where every mile marker is another doom-and-gloom sign. God wants your thinking to be wholesome, positive and looking for the return of Jesus.

April Makes a Break for It

For this is the love of God, that we keep his commandments: and his commandments are not grievous. John 5:3

April is one of our dogs and being a beagle, she is all hound dog. She holds a special place in my heart; although, at times, she can really get on my nerves. Because she is a hound dog, her nose often leads her. Therefore, she must remain on a leash because any wild scent will draw her into the woods.

A few days ago, she seized an opportunity to make her escape into the world. Seizing her new freedom with all the gusto of a healthy hound, she made a beeline for the woods and as far away from home as possible. There was a world to see and rabbits to chase! She was now going to do as she pleased!

What April did not know was that she left the confine of free food, love, and protection. She, like a lot of people, did not recognize the safety and blessings of living within borders – within limits.

Many rebel against God's principles for the "do-as-I-please" life without considering the consequences of living outside those principles. God didn't give us boundaries to make us unhappy. He gave us rules, principles, to help us live a life of joy, peace, and safety.

Like the prodigal son, April came to her senses and made the same discovery that Dorothy did – "there's no place like home." Although there was a season of joy by running wild in the woods, the forest was also scary and dangerous; and the food wasn't free.

Perhaps you have found yourself longing to "break loose!" Take a little advice from a hound dog! Enjoy the freedom you have by living within the boundaries of God's love. Hoever, should you be one of those who have chosen the "do-as-I-please" life, the Father is waiting with open arms. True freedom is found within God's boundaries.

Danger Thin Air

The view from the mountain top can be wonderfully but anyone who has climbed mountains can tell you that the higher the mountain the thinner the air. Revivals, conferences, retreats, and camp meetings can put you on a spiritual mountain top but beware of the danger of thin air caused by experiences.

While you are caught up in the glory of the experience, the devil wants to take your breath away! The devil doesn't see the wonder of the mountaintop experience. He sees the mountaintop experience as an opportunity to cause you to have a great fall. Be on your guard because spiritual highs can descend into spiritual valleys.

The mountaintop experience can give us a glimpse into heaven, and that is great; but while our heart and head are in the clouds, our feet must be firmly planted on the one who made the mountain. Thank God, our faith and joy do not depend upon experiences but on truth.

Choose to Think Good!

Think about things that are true like the love of God! Let your thoughts be about things that are lovely like the beauty of creation.

Choose not to think about darkness, problems, or negative possibilities. Do not let the devil choose where your thoughts go. Choose to let your thoughts be positive and see the glory of God working in your life.

Finally, brethren, whatsoever things are true, whatsoever things are honest, whatsoever things are just, whatsoever things are pure, whatsoever things are lovely, whatsoever things are of good report; if there be any virtue, and if there be any praise, think on these things. (Philippians 4:8)

Are You In a Hard Way?

The Psalmist of the seventy-seventh Psalms is in a hard way. "In the day of my trouble I sought the Lord: my sore ran in the night, and ceased not: my soul refused to be comforted" (v2). He sought peace but could not find it until he remembered that God is the one who does miracles (v.14) and remembered how the Lord had delivered his people from a really tough spot by parting the Red Sea. He brings to a conclusion his thought in the nineteenth verse: "Your path led through the sea, your way through the mighty waters, though your footprints were not seen" (NIV).

God's way led the people of Israel though perhaps the scariest path of all – two walls of water! Although they could not see his footprints leading them, he was none the less! Often we can make it through the tough times of life because we can see the footprints of Jesus leading us. However, it is those times when there are no footprints that demand faith.

Walking by faith can be tough. However, you can take heart. The Good Shepherd is still leading the way.

Roll with the punches

Roll with the punches. Everyone on this journey we call life will find that life can throw some very hard punches. The secret to living a full life is to roll with punches. You may be knocked down, but you are not knocked out until this life ends. Absorb the difficulty with the attitude that tomorrow is a new day – a new opportunity.

Persecuted, but not forsaken; cast down, but not destroyed; 2Co 4:9

Clear the Table

My wife has a pet-peeve. She likes for her kitchen table to be clear without exception. Of course, the kitchen table is the first place everyone drops things, so my wife is usually stewing over her table. However, with the New Year beginning and a compelling need to make new resolutions, I thought it would be nice to resolve myself to relieve my honey of stress and attempt to keep the table clean and neat. (Actually, my first thought was to remove the table but realized that would only develop a more stressed wife.)

After giving some thought to developing a habit of keeping the kitchen table clean, it struck me that perhaps I should clear my life-table. Surely, you have heard and possibly said, "I have too much on my table, or I have too much on my plate." Well, I have too much on my life-plate; and perhaps you do too.

Things have become cluttered and overlapping. The urgent is crowding out the important and work is overwhelming and not any fun. I am becoming a grumpy old man. It's time to reevaluate and dismiss some of the clutter.

The question is, "Where do I start?" The following is a few of my thoughts and resolutions. Some you may wish to make!

- I am going to add a new word to my vocabulary. The word is NO. I am not going to take on more than I should and excuse my actions by saying, "No one else will do it" or "It's easier if I just do it myself."

- I am going to spend more of my time in prayer. My table becomes full when I undertake that which is not of the Lord. By God's grace, I will accept and accomplish only those tasks he gives me; and by His grace, I will learn to wait for his timing. I will know His will by seeking it through prayer.
- I am going to focus on one task at a time. Multitasking is not my thing. I will excel at that which I undertake. I will, with God's help, see each task to the end.
- I am going to lay to rest, with God's help, the following weights that hold me down and keep me from accomplishing God's will for my life: Pride, anger, worry, fear, and doubt.
    - By the power of the Spirit, I will not let my injured pride clutter my life-table with unsettled issues; but I will walk in meekness and nurture a humble spirit.
    - By the power of God's love, I will shed the weight of anger and adopt a spirit of forgiveness and reconciliation.
    - Because of God's faithfulness, I will not worry but walk by faith.
    - Because of the character and attributes of God, I will not let fear hinder or stop me. I will do the work of the Lord with confidence and assurance; and I will not doubt. I will be victorious!

    My table will be clear of pride, anger, worry, fear, and doubt.
- I recognize that to clear my life-table, I must weigh my words. I must address others with care. I must not speak badly of others. I must speak only the truth. Too much time and energy have been spent in the past retracing and retracting my words. I will need godly wisdom if I am to weigh my words.

- I will see problems as opportunities. I will grow because of problems and will seek to learn from problems. I will not procrastinate when approached with problems but will seek to resolve each problem with God's help. I will not allow problems to clutter my life-table.
- I will continue to fall deeply in love with my Lord, my wife, my children, my family, my church family, my brothers and sisters in Christ. I will learn to love even my enemies. I can do so because God first loved me.

Cricket Jitters

Toby, our pup, has found that he likes the taste of crickets. This has the cricket community up in arms as they scurry to find a way to combat a playful pup that is on the constant hunt for a tasty treat. Have no fear; the crickets have found a weak spot!

While Toby is a ferocious foe and is a thousand times larger than even the biggest cricket, he is terribly afraid of any crawly thing landing on his bottom. This summer has been extremely painful for Toby, who has found that sitting on bees is not a very wise thing. Since experiencing this twice, Toby has been excessively careful about letting anything touch his back end.

Our little cricket friends have learned that if just one of them will hop on the back end of this villain dog, they can cause this puppy to run for the house. Of course, the cricket on the tail gets the ride of his life, but he saved many friends from becoming dog food.

Isn't it amazing how the little things can cause us to run and hide? For example, let someone hurt our feelings at church or someone criticize our work, and we'll get into the run-for-the-house mode every time. "I'll never go back to that church! See if I ever do anything again!" Some hurtful remark stings us and then we're afraid of every little bug that comes our way.

It should not be that way! We are wiser than a puppy. Aren't we?

Be kind and compassionate to one another, forgiving each other, just as in Christ God forgave you. Ephesians 4:32 (NIV)

Seven principles of discernment

Discerning between what is right and what is wrong can be difficult when the Bible doesn't address a choice directly. *Use the following questions to find God's will for every area of your life!*

- **Does it appear evil?**

    Abstain from all appearances of evil. -1 Thessalonians 5:22

- **Does it give a foothold to the Devil?**

    Neither give place to the devil. - Ephesians 4:27

- **Will it cause someone to sin?**

    Let us not therefore judge one another any more: but judge this rather, that no man put a stumblingblock or an occasion to fall in his brother's way. - Romans 14:13

    But take heed lest by any means this liberty of yours become a stumblingblock to them that are weak.
    -1 Corinthians 8:9

- **Is it the right thing to do?**

    Therefore to him that knoweth to do good, and doeth it not, to him it is sin. - James 4:17

    All things are lawful for me, but all things are not expedient... -1 Corinthians 10:23

Continued

- **Does it build up or tear down others?**

  All things are lawful for me, but all things are not expedient: all things are lawful for me, but all things edify not. -1 Corinthians 10:23

  Let us therefore follow after the things which make for peace, and things wherewith one may edify another. -Romans 14:19

- **How does it affect your heart?**

  Keep thy heart with all diligence; for out of it are the issues of life. - Proverbs 4:23

- **Will you have a clear conscience?**

  Beloved, if our heart condemn us not, then have we confidence toward God. -1 John 3:21

  Having a good conscience... 1 Peter 3:16

Seek Counsel

No one has a handle on everything! Before making major decisions in any area of life seek the counsel of those that have knowledge in that area. Don't seek counsel from a brain surgeon to fix your car or from a mechanic about a brain tumor. Likewise, do not seek spiritual guidance from someone who is not walking with the Lord. And! Always remember that the true expert in every area of your life is the Lord. Always seek the Lord's counsel!

Bully Fish

In the little corner of the house that I call my office, among the mess of papers, books, and an overworked computer, is an aquarium. Although I often neglect this aquarium, it has managed to keep three African Cichlids alive for over a year. Amazing not only because of the lack of care but because African Cichlids are bullies and mean by nature. They are so aggressive that few other fish can live with them in the confines of an aquarium. They are constantly nipping at each other.

Unfortunately, the aquarium and the fish often bear a resemblance to some homes and some church families. Some homes are in a constant state of war with each member nipping away at the other members. The same can be true for many church families.

The family and the church should be the two places where people are engulfed with love and find peace.

A new commandment I give unto you, That ye love one another; as I have loved you, that ye also love one another. (John 13:34)

A Prayer

Allow me Lord to be a beacon of love. Where there is hatred let me show love. Cleanse me of bitterness, prejudice, and thoughts of revenge. Allow me to be a vessel of love. Help me to deeply love my family, my friends, my neighbors, and my enemies; and Lord let my love for you continually grow. Amen.

April Wants to Talk

April, the lovable beagle that has won our hearts with her antics, has many good traits. She is loyal, friendly, and desires to please. She has one annoying characteristic that wipes out the others in an instant. Her bark would, if possible, wake the dead! And bark, she does for just about anything she wants. You see, April can't talk but wants to talk!

We usually have no idea what April is trying to tell us. Sometimes she wants out. Often, she wants water while at other times she wants everyone to go to bed. She just doesn't have the ability to tell us exactly what she wants. However, she continues to try with great effort much to our displeasure and her frustration.

Fortunately, when it comes to communicating with our spouses, children, or others, we can talk. Unfortunately, we often resort to April's method of communicating. We bark!

Frequently what we call talking is nothing more than a series of snarls and barks. The husband barks his orders to the wife. She in return growls back. And the kids – they learn from the parents.

Some places of employment aren't any different. The boss growls the employee snarls, and very little productive communication takes place.

Sadly, this manner of communication can also be found in the church.

It appears that while April, our dog, would like to talk and can't; people can talk but choose to bark.

Perhaps today would be a good day for all of us to consider how we are communicating and try to do a little more talking and a little less barking.

A soft answer turneth away wrath: but grievous words stir up anger. (Proverbs 15:1)

> *Through patience a ruler can be persuaded, and a gentle tongue can break a bone.*
> Proverbs 25:15

Don't Attract the Mosquitoes

Summertime brings green leaves and pretty flowers, but it also brings those little vampires commonly known as mosquitoes.

Several years ago I preached a youth camp in Michigan where the mosquitoes competed with most small birds. Everyone spent much of their days and nights swatting the blood-sucking hordes that never seemed to cease to invade the cabins.

That year I learned a valuable lesson concerning mosquitoes and life. The old camp director told us that the best way to avoid the vampire attacks was not to wear anything that would attract them. It seems that mosquitoes are more attracted to aftershave lotion than are the ladies. Perfumed soap, deodorant, and shampoo call out to mosquitoes like raw meat does to a lion. I quickly learned that odorless was fine. However, the teens were a little slower adapting.

You see youth camp for teens is more about scoping out the girls and the guys than anything else. For the gals to go without that sweet-smelling makeup or the guys to go without the latest babe-drawing cologne would have been the end of the world.

That brings me to the life lesson. In an attempt to attract the attention of someone else we can also attract the attention of those maggots we don't want. Both gals and guys must take care when it comes to dressing modestly. Obviously, a person wants to present themselves in the best light; but if you are attracting more mosquitoes than foxes, then perhaps you need to take a second look at how you are presenting yourself. Any dog will drool over a piece of meat but only a disciplined man or woman can appreciate a work of art. Present yourself as a work of art and not a piece of meat.

If You Hang Out A Bird Feeder

> *If you judge people you have no time to love them.*
> —Mother Teresa

I was admiring several yellow finches feasting at my bird feeder when they came. Big blackbirds swooped down scaring my little songbirds away and gobbling up the goodies. How dare those bullies! I reached for the broom ready to go to battle when the truth smacked me. If you hang out a bird feeder, you can expect all kinds of birds.

As simple as this truth is, it is none-the-less forgotten by the church. If you hang out the bread of life, then expect more than just the nice people to gather around it. We forget that the gospel is not just for those that dress like us, look like us, and embrace all the things we do. The gospel is for all – even the blackbirds.

There is one way to rid yourself of the blackbirds. Don't hang the bird feeder out. Of course, you won't attract any songbirds either.

For ye are bought with a price: therefore glorify God in your body, and in your spirit, which are God's. -1 Corinthians 6:20

> *Then Peter opened his mouth, and said, Of a truth I perceive that God is no respecter of persons:* -Acts 10:34
>
> *For there is no respect of persons with God.* -Romans 2:11

Unity & Humbleness

The early church weathered many a major life-storm in its beginning. Persecuted by Jewish leaders and blessed by God with an unprecedented flood of new believers, the early church leaned heavy on prayer, unity, and humbleness of spirit.

A quick study of the book of Acts would reveal a prayerful mixed band of believers that followed the example of their Lord by praying often and gathering together to face the challenges of the day. The true maturity of a church is not found in the age of its members or in the number of believers but in the unity of its members – unity in the cause, in faith, and in PRAYER.

- **Every Christian is unified in the cause of Christ:**

    "Thy kingdom come. Thy will be done in earth, as it is in heaven" (Matthew 6:10).

- **Every Christian is unified in faith – faith in the person of Jesus the Christ:**

    "Neither is there salvation in any other: for there is none other name under heaven given among men, whereby we must be saved" (Acts 4:12).

- **Every Christian is united by prayer:**

    "…pray one for another…" (James 5:16)

Why Do Squirrels Play in the Road?

If you were coming from the north, you would travel down a back-road through a state forest to get to my house. It is a very pretty drive anytime of the year. It is also the playground for many squirrels, which brings me to my question: Why do squires play in the road?

It is obvious that such action is dangerous and from the numerous near misses you would think the squirrels would learn to stay off the road! Nevertheless, every day there they are again!

I am sure there is some federal grant money out there and some elite professor has done a study on this phenomenon. However, this risky behavior can also be seen in ordinary people every day! Foolish people are playing with drugs, alcohol, tobacco, and permissive sex. I have no scientific statistics to proof this, but it would not surprise me that more people die from their risky behavior than squirrels do from playing on the road.

There is an answer to the question why people enter into such risky behavior, and it's found in the Bible!

- The way of a fool is right in his own eyes… (Proverbs 12:15)

- There is a way which seemeth right unto a man, but the end thereof are the ways of death. (Proverbs 14:12)

Foolish people ignore or deny God and heed not to the warnings and precepts found in the Bible. They play with behavior that is as deadly as squirrels playing in the road.

The Wow in Jesus' Healing

Jesus saith unto him, Thomas, because thou hast seen me, thou hast believed: blessed are they that have not seen, and yet have believed. And many other signs truly did Jesus in the presence of his disciples, which are not written in this book: But these are written, that ye might believe that Jesus is the Christ, the Son of God; and that believing ye might have life through his name. John 20:29-31

For we know that the whole creation groaneth and travaileth in pain together until now. -Romans 8:22

Philip Yancey's book *The Jesus I Never Knew* was one of many books that I had only partially read. I started it shortly after reading his *What's So Amazing About Grace* and lost interest about halfway through the book in the chapter on – yes grace. I think I had heard about all I could about grace from Yancey at that point. That was a big mistake.

Several days ago I picked up *The Jesus I Never Knew* and starting reading the next chapter, which is about Jesus' miracles. Yancey struck a spiritual cord with me as he introduced his thoughts on Jesus' miracles of healing concluding with this wonderful point:

> *"...it was in Jesus' nature to counteract the effects of the fallen world during his time on earth. As he strode through life Jesus used supernatural power to set right what was wrong."*

Jesus is still setting things right! That is the Wow in Jesus' Healing!

Influence!

The dictionary defines influence as the capacity or power of persons or things to be a compelling force on or produce effects on the actions, behavior, opinions, etc., of others.

Influence! We all have it to some degree or another, sometimes in a positive manner and often in a negative manner. Influence is always at play, whether we are aware of it or not. On occasion, the most casual contact or word can have the greatest impact. Strangely, we never know what contact or what word or what action will have the most influence nor do we know when nor how.

Take for an example the Apostle Paul singing songs of praise to the Lord while imprisoned. That faithfulness, that witness would have a great influence on the jailer. John F. Walvoord would comment on Paul's influence in his commentary on Philippians:

> *One effect of Paul's faithfulness and consistent witness was that "many," literally, "the greater number" of the brethren in the Lord were made more bold to speak the Word without fear. If Paul could preach in prison fearlessly, they could preach the Word outside prison. His influence was such that the greater majority of Christians in Rome were encouraged to witness"* (Philippians Triumph in Christ, p.38).

While it is true, we live our life for Christ and not for others, we must never lose sight of the fact that our influence is far reaching.

May Our Lord allow our influence to be positive and may it point others to Jesus.

Hope in a Dark World

After John was put in prison, Jesus went into Galilee, proclaiming the good news of God. Mark 1:14 (NIV)

The first words spoken by our Lord, as recorded in the gospel of Mark, highlight the gospel message of the New Testament. They are bright words of hope painted on a backdrop of despair. John's ministry was abruptly brought to an end. The voice of truth was silenced by those who had no intention of repenting. They only dabbled in religion because of curiosity. The believer should always beware of such people because they are not your friends.

John had cleared the path and prepared the people for the message of hope. Now Jesus began, in earnest, proclaiming this message of hope that the world needed. The Messiah was here, and God's Kingdom was near!

What was necessary for people to receive this message?

Repent and believe!

Literally, the word "repent" means to change one's mind. It has the idea of changing ones complete "mind set." It means to change your entire attitude about literally everything and especially about sin. Repentance is both a heart change and a mind change. It causes people to make a 180-degree turn. Anything less is not biblical repentance.

The second element in Jesus' message of hope is that of faith or believing. Believing the message means you must believe the messenger. Jesus announces a radical change from the law, which continually condemned people, to the hope of grace. For the people of Jesus' time and for the people of our time, this is completely contradictory of what is embraced by the world. To even partially understand grace and especially to receive grace, you must believe the messenger, Jesus. He is the good news. He is the gospel.

Recklessness and Faith

George Armstrong rose up the army ranks quickly and was known for his bravery among his men and his superiors. Fighting for the Union, George's bravery bordered on recklessness. During the Civil War, he managed to have eleven horses shot out from under him. His passion, zeal, and recklessness would catch up with him in 1876 when General George Armstrong Custer would lose his life at thirty-six.

There is a fine line between faith and foolishness, bravery and recklessness, and between courage and wisdom. Many have forgotten to seek the wisdom of the Lord before stepping out on faith or has allowed their zeal cloud their decisions. Take, for example, Jephthah, who made a foolish vow to the Lord and ended up sacrificing his daughter (see Judges 11).

Although God wants His children to be brave and courageous, he does not want them to be foolish and unwise. Walking by faith can, at times, be tricky. It is always best to spend time in prayer and test your decisions and actions with the Word of God.

All the Days in the World?

In Mitch Albom's little book, *The Five People You Meet In Heaven*, there are these lines:

> "Had he known his death was imminent, he might have gone somewhere else. Instead, he did what we all do. He went about his dull routine as if all the days in the world were still to come." (p. 4)

Indeed, we do go about our life "as if all the days in the world were still to come." The bible, however, warns us against such a mindset and cautions us against such an assumption. The Psalmist cried to the Lord, "So teach us to number our days, that we may apply our hearts unto wisdom" (Ps 90:12). And again, the Bible says in the Psalms, "LORD, make me to know mine end, and the measure of my days, what it is; that I may know how frail I am" (Ps 39:4). In fact, we are encouraged to "Redeeming the time, because the days are evil (Eph 5:16).

One does wonder what our life would be like if we approached everyday as our last day?

> ### When Life on Earth Ends
>
> *When I put my head down to rest for one last time on earth, allow me to do so knowing your love and forgiveness Lord Jesus. May the words I hear when I enter your presence be "Well done."*
> *Jim Barr, Your Servant*

Now the God of peace, that brought again from the dead our Lord Jesus, that great shepherd of the sheep, through the blood of the everlasting covenant, Make you perfect in every good work to do his will, working in you that which is wellpleasing in his sight, through Jesus Christ; to whom be glory for ever and ever. Amen.

Hebrew 13: 20-21

About the Author

James (Jim) Barr makes his home in the Hoosier State of Indiana with his wife, Pat, and two very spoiled dogs. Having served in the ministry of the Lord for almost forty years as pastor and missionary, he is now retired and currently striving to fulfill his "bucket-list" of which *For His Glory* topped his list.

Pastor Jim delights in encouraging and equipping the local church for today's changing ministry. He is available for speaking and teaching appoints as the Lord leads. He may be contacted by email at **pastorjimbarr@gmail.com**.

Pastor Jim is also an avid internet blogger and offers devotional thoughts as well as teaching materials at his website **www.net153.com**. You may also follow Pastor Jim on Facebook and Twitter. Links are avail at his website.

Made in the USA
Lexington, KY
27 December 2011